W9-BMZ-179

The Fluid Boundaries of Suffrage and Jim Crow

The Fluid Boundaries of Suffrage and Jim Crow

Staking Claims in the American Heartland

Edited by DaMaris B. Hill

LEXINGTON BOOKS
Lanham • Boulder • New York • London

Published by Lexington Books
An imprint of The Rowman & Littlefield Publishing Group, Inc.
4501 Forbes Boulevard, Suite 200, Lanham, Maryland 20706
www.rowman.com

Unit A, Whitacre Mews, 26-34 Stannary Street, London SE11 4AB

Copyright © 2016 by Lexington Books

All rights reserved. No part of this book may be reproduced in any form or by any
electronic or mechanical means, including information storage and retrieval systems,
without written permission from the publisher, except by a reviewer who may quote
passages in a review.

British Library Cataloguing in Publication Information Available

Library of Congress Cataloging-in-Publication Data

Hill, DaMaris B., editor.
The fluid boundaries of suffrage and Jim Crow : staking claims in the American heartland / by
    DaMaris B. Hill.
Lanham : Lexington Books, 2016. | Includes bibliographical references and index.
LCCN 2015051176 (print) | LCCN 2016006169 (ebook) | ISBN 9780739197875 (cloth : alk. paper) |
    ISBN 9780739197882 (Electronic)
LCSH: United States--Race relations--History--20th century. | African Americans--Social condi-
    tions--20th century.
LCC E185.61 .F635 2016 (print) | LCC E185.61 (ebook) | DDC 305.80097309/04--dc23
LC record available at http://lccn.loc.gov/2015051176

∞™ The paper used in this publication meets the minimum requirements of American
National Standard for Information Sciences Permanence of Paper for Printed Library
Materials, ANSI/NISO Z39.48-1992.

Printed in the United States of America

Contents

Introduction

DaMaris B. Hill

In December 2012, NPR's Mary Sharratt wrote an article entitled "Time Passages: The Year's Best Historical Fiction." Wherein she states, "like all great literature, the best historical fiction must have something meaningful to say, some insight that is ultimately timeless." As a literary artist, my most recent work is a collection entitled *Willows of the Spring*. This series of novels is about society's struggles to control the sexuality of young women in the Plains Region during the 1930s. The novel and associated research is interdisciplinary and contextualizes the oppressions and opportunities resulting from the Suffrage Movement in the Heartland. This book, *The Fluid Boundaries of Suffrage and Jim Crow*, is an edited collection of essays that will explore the intersections of Suffrage, race relations, and cultural memories/histories against the backdrop of Midwestern culture during the early part of the twentieth century America's Heartland. Lawrence Buell's theories about environmental memory remind us that up to a point, world history of space becoming place.[1] This collection aims to further examine regional histories and the ways collective memories of spaces influence the remembering of these spaces. Chapters from this edited volume add to an ongoing dialogue about representations of gender and race within the context of regional and national histories.

This book enters an important conversation about race relations in the early part of the twentieth century. When exploring regional and national histories, one must acknowledge the extreme instances racial and gendered oppression in the Heartland are often overshadowed by the economic collapse that altered the reality of many of the capitalist icons, America's social elite. Edward Said theories suggest that memory and its representations touch significantly upon questions of identity, nationalism, power, and authority. Far from being neutral exercise in facts and basic truths, the study of history, which of course is an underpinning of memory, both in school and university, is to some considerable extant a nationalist effort premised on the need to construct a desirable loyalty to and insider's understanding of one's country, tradition and faith.[2] The historical narrative regarding this time period is over simplified; the stories of "the people" are absent. Even within the discussion of Jim Crow and race relations, there is an over simplified and reductive historical narrative regarding gender. The over simplification and reduction of the racial and gender inequalities associated with this historical era has resulted in a erasure of the long history of the Civil Rights Movement and tensions that significantly contributed with the defensive political ideologies expressed in the Black Nationalist Movement, subsequent the culture wars. Discussing place often seems to offer the promise of a politics of resistance.[3] These narratives extend Heartland histories beyond the promises of the American Creed into specific histories that discuss race and gender.

Embodied testimonies and collective memory, they are important aspects of these interpretations of the Heartland. It is also important to examine how the American Creed intersects with embodied histories and collective ways of knowing and remembering. In the dominant culture's memory, the Heartland is a geographic space and the destination of the American Promise and therefore beholden to the American Creed. The American Creed, rooted in the Declaration of Independence, expresses core political values that include liberty, equality, individualism, democracy, and the rule of the law under the constitution.[4]

Considering how the "Heartland" was promoted and the ways it manifests in the American Creed and psyche, interpreting the multiple cultural histories of the "Heartland" region and their respective intersections are vital for understanding the ways people perceive new "cultural" geographies and environmental memory. It is at the crossroads of race and gender, subjectivity and collectivity, that my creative and intellectual power is embodied, remembered and rendered. Some of the ways I conceived of this project are in conversation with the promises associated with the American Creed.

The chapters in this collection are in conversation with pioneering the frontier and freedom manifest in collective identity and the cultural memory of the Heartland. When I was envisioning this project, I was also curious about how systematic racism and political movements such as Suffrage historically influence the geographical spaces of the Heartland. I also questioned how embodied identity and associated acts of violence influenced and/or disrupted the American Creed.

This collection requires thinking more rigorously about place as physical environment whether mainly "built" or "national" constituted simultaneously by subjective perception and by institutionalized social arrangements.[5] In a speech dated October 27, 2008, Lawrence Buell states that he is in the early stages of accessing how artistic acts, literature especially for his purposes, create environmental memory . . . [meaning an] awareness whether idiosyncratic or socially shared.[6] As a student of Lawrence Buell, I explored the four individual aspects of environmental memory categorized as social, cultural, spatial (architecture/manmade and natural), and collective identities. According to Buell, environmental studies encourages readers to discover and critically investigate the intersections between collective memory, individual agency, physical environment, and notions of place. This field of study challenges academics and readers to consider the eco-psychological pragmatics that disrupts our "knowing" of spaces. Buell also goes on to say that Environmental criticism must also confront the proposition that "non-places are the real measure of our time."[7] How do spaces become defined in terms of capture and exclusion and how do these knowings of spaces connect to the chapters in this book? Traditions of storytelling aggregate captured human experiences, just as these captured moments enable institutions of human storytelling.[8]

WHAT AND WHERE IS AMERICA'S HEARTLAND?

Geographically, the "Heartland" of the United States is conceptualized as the Union states of Middle America, the states that did not touch either of the oceans that frame the nation's borders. As an "imagined geography," the Heartland has come to be recognized as the Midwestern and Bible states of America, those states with politically conservative leanings and fundamental Christian values that are affirmed in the secular epithetical values of the American Creed.[9] For the purposes of this edited collection, I conceive the Heartland to be the states that do not border any oceans and embody the multiple histories of the American frontier. This collection illustrates how Heartland histories remain fluid, because of the influences of migration, identity and cultural memories associated with these spaces. The chapters also engage directly and explicitly with the ways race, gender, and intersectional identities are remembered, expressed, and contextualized in the Heartland. Specifically, this work shows how utopian ideals and propaganda associated with American Creed impacted collective memories rooted in contemporary notions of identity in the Heartland.

Because imagining a place with any fullness requires at least a glimpse of its whole history, this book focuses on the way national histories and dominant culture remembers the Heartland. In kind the conflation between American identity, Westward expansion and the wilderness or frontier as the manifestation of freedom, the Heartland spaces was viewed as the ideal space for communal Utopias. Ultimately the wilderness frontier came to represent the "unknown, the disordered, the dangerous" and subsequently a "moral and physical wasteland fit only for conquest and transformation in the name of progress, civilization, and Christianity." In the name of expansion and pioneering, capitalist goals had to make mass religious narrative associated with Eden and paradise "tamed" and "owned" and/or otherwise reconfigured as Christian paradise in order to be secularly consumed.[10] Wilderness had no place in the American version of the paradise myth.[11] Much like the original Northwest territories of Ohio, Indiana, Illinois, Michigan, and Wisconsin, the Heartland inclusive of the Plains region became a geographic space filled with sentiments of opportunity layered into notions of the pioneering spirit. Along with the American Creed, the pioneering spirit helped to inspire versions of utopian ideals into the people seeking to occupy that space. This sentiment was encouraged in the establishment of the Kansas-Nebraska Territory, wherein Senator Douglas proposed "popular sovereignty"[12] as a solution to the debate over whether the territory should enter as a free territory or one that allowed slavery.

NOSTALGIA AND LEGACIES OF THE NINETEENTH CENTURY

The early part of the Twentieth century was revealed in the excitement of the industrial revolution. The United States of America enjoyed a bolstering economy that promised to transform the work of individuals in the agricultural sector. In kind, the Heartland was a space of economic diversity that had strongholds in both the agricultural and industrial sectors. The Heartland promised the stability necessary to sustain agricultural and industrialized economies. This fact coupled with the optimism associated with the westward expansion, the Heartland experienced mass migrations during the late Nineteenth century and the early Twentieth. It became a refuge for those transitioning from the agricultural economies domestically from the southern states and internationally. The region largely benefited from the human resources and individual contributions of people abandoning the South. This migration, the southern trade drain, was comprised of individuals and families who sought to recover from the economic disappointment and displacement associated in a post-Civil War culture. In kind after the Civil War some residents of the Old Northwest continued their westward migration . . . they were joined by immigrants from Sweden, Norway, and the Ukraine. The Heartland is most significant also because this is where ideas and sentiments of utopianism thrived.[13] Each migrant community brought with them utopic visions of ideal societies, paradise, which were affirmed in the ways these communities interpreted the American Dream and associated American Creed. The members of this new society sought to redefine and secure a collective foothold in the world, and then announce that they had the truth.[14]

    The utopian fever was applied in many contexts that broadly and subsequently reflected the values of the American Creed in political and religious contexts. These ideas were borrowed heavily from the Christian myths. The capitalist imperatives associated with the westward expansion necessitated that these myths be "tamed" and "owned," or otherwise reconfigured as a (Christian) paradise in order to be secularly consumed.[15] The evangelical sermons of this era chronicled the "End of Days." Likewise, they presented moral and ethical ideals as "Last Chance" opportunities for individuals to earn their way into Heaven. Soon the Christian rhetoric and connotations for paradise and utopia were applied to political contexts. Theodore Roosevelt's speech illustrates these connections.

On August 31, 1910, President Theodore Roosevelt gave a speech in Osawatomie, Kansas, entitled "New Nationalism." "New Nationalism" came to stand for a strong military and global presence but also nationalization of life generally.[16] Roosevelt's notions of "New Nationalism" stand not only for a strong military and global presence but also nationalization of life generally.[17] Many believe that this speech was written in the wake of Roosevelt reading Herbert Croly's *The Promise of American Life*, deemed the Progressive-Era's bible.[18] In this speech, Roosevelt calls for the Progressive revolution in politics, economics, and civil society, stating:

> The essence of any struggle for healthy liberty has always been, and must always be, to take from some one man or class of men the right to enjoy power, or wealth, or position, or immunity, which has not been earned by service to his or their fellows. That is what you fought for in the Civil War, and that is what we strive for now.[19]

Roosevelt's overlapping his message of a new type of nationalism with special attention to Kansas' abolition history was also expressed in his speech. Roosevelt's speech made it a point to quote Lincoln and to celebrate the John Brown. In the speech Roosevelt seems to understate any sentiments pertaining to popular sovereignty or the legacy of racism associated with chattel forms of slavery. The promises of popular sovereignty and slavery remained in the collective memory of the Kansas residents that envisioned the Heartland as a utopic place that valued abolition and the values of the Republican Party.

Although the Heartland was not completely occupied by utopian communities, the ideas and common beliefs that are present in both secular and religious utopias promoted individual bonds that formed larger communities in this space. Similar to Pilgrim, Calvert, and Quaker communities that were unified by a common faith in the early colonies, the secular utopic communities embraced ideas that included "the alleviation of financial or social distress." In some cases, the secular utopias promised the elimination of the dehumanizing condition of factory work and at the same time provided security, fraternity, a better education, and moral improvement through communal living.[20]

Comprised of Asian, Indigenous, Mexican, African, European, Anglo American, and African American people, the Heartland had various interpretations of paradise and ideas of utopia. The various versions of utopia were rooted in the collective memories of groups and their respective interpretations of America's Creed. In another example, African American communities such as the Exodusters sought spaces and communities that were free of the racialized violence and exploitation many experienced in established eastern communities. The Exodusters also sought to build communities of racial solidarity, because this utopian community believed that without racial solidarity the race could never progress.[21]

Whereas Sutton questions when and why people sought to establish utopic communities in the Heartland, I suspect the possibility of the federal push for eugenic politics and policies stimulated for some and affirmed for others, the desire for monolithic communities and social divisions based on race. I also explore the possibility that these eugenic ideas were coupled with the intense public education campaigns created a nuevo and progressive collective consciousness. Some Heartlanders may have viewed their individual and collective identity as the manifestation of New Nationalism and a reflection of a central region that is "politically, economically, or militarily vital to a nation."[22] This new nationalist identity used the rhetoric of equality to frame their respective utopian ideas rooted in identity. The term "Native American" was a popular marker of identity among white Americans that identified with being descendants of the first colonists and settlers of New England.[23] While this new nationalism campaign reinforced the American Creed and encouraged a nationalist identity, public campaigns rooted in the pseudo-science of eugenics created hierarchies that worked against any of the liberatory and progressive promises of equally expressed in the "New Nationalism" speech.

Eugenic science is largely understood as the improvement of the inborn qualities, or stock, of the human population.[24] With a heightened awareness and promotion of eugenic science in the public sphere, the influence of eugenic propaganda was pervasive in the highest forms of government and the smallest nuclear families. The emergent pseudo-science of eugenics validated anxieties rooted in racism, class bias, and anti-immigrant sentiments in Heartland communities. Despite the fact that eugenic theories proved to be racist, sexist, and classist, many religious and civic organizations promoted the theories. The pseudo-scientific theories were adapted as truth by influential institutions, such as the Carnegie Institution of Washington, and civic leaders, such as Alexander Graham Bell. An intense public education campaign, bolstered by religious and public sectors, propelled eugenic science into the mainstream culture within a few short years. American culture, inclusive of regional spaces such as the Heartland, embedded such knowledge into the collective consciousness and memory of its citizens. Embers of these ideas are still evident in popular culture and some academic discourses.

In *Heartland Utopias*, Sutton questions why some utopias were not sustainable. Many of the essays in this collection show that the stability of the Heartland communities was threatened segregation and racial exclusion. The separatists and racial ideologies were inspired by and affirmed within eugenic policies that framed political agenda on state and federal levels. The federal push for Eugenic policies was coupled with the intense public education campaigns created a collective consciousness in the public sphere, including utopian communities that had previously established communal principles. In kind, theses pseudo-scientific eugenic policies threatened the stability of communities that were comprised of various ethnic identities by introducing ideas of criminality and bias rooted in racial and ethnic differences. For example many African American people sought utopia in the Heartland spaces, but were unable actualize this ideal community because assimilation into racially diverse utopic societies often asked members to adopt the ideologies present in eugenic sciences, despite the fact that eugenic ideologies compromised on the tenants of liberty, equality, individuality, and democracy. Such ideologies contrasted with the American creed and personal motivation to join such communities. Exoduster movement leader "Pap" Singleton advocated for a mass exodus of blacks from Tennessee, where the Black masses played a less active political role, to Kansas. In Singleton's view, proper public action sprang from divine revelation, not from the democratic process.[25] Similarly, immigrants experienced challenges when attempting to join utopian communities that existed in the Heartland. In this particular instance, assimilation is another kid of violence that can be embodied, assimilating alienation, ones own as well as others.[26] Contrary to the values asserted in the American Creed, utopian communities valued assimilation communal practices over individuality and equality, often at the expense of ideas pertaining to democracy.

This collection employs theories associated with environmental and cultural memories in order to explore the promises of freedom that the Heartland frontiers proposed in the early twentieth century. Because the public eugenic campaigns were so popular, it is important to examine how hierarchal reasoning intersected with cultural/political ideologies such as Suffrage and Jim Crow. It is also important to recognize that the Heartland culture assumes a posture of ethnocentricity. This means that Heartland culture embraces America as a monolithic culture with an English heritage of some of the first colonists. These colonists were referred to as "Native Americans" in this era. As a result, many believed that all Heartland ethnicities should express values that are rooted in a monolithic Anglo-American ethnic identity that reflects English heritage. In order to enter a dialogue about these assumptions about the Heartland, this collection aims to ask questions such as:

- How are promises associated with the American Dream and values of the American Creed, particularly pioneering and the ideas of "freedom" associated with democracy, conflate and collide with ethnocentricity and in the cultural memory of the Heartland?
- How did gendered political movements such as Suffrage historically influence the demographic and political landscape of the Heartland?
- How did instances of violence rooted in racism and Jim Crow policies conflict, impact and diversify the opportunities and collective narratives about the Heartland?

This work intends in some ways to expand the research of Wanda Hendricks in her book *Gender, race, and politics in the Midwest: Black club women in Illinois* (1998) by introducing narratives about the experiences of club women in the Heartland states. Similarly to Glenda Gilmore's *Gender and Jim Crow: Women and the Politics of White Supremacy in North Carolina, 1896–1920*, (1996) the work will enter a dialogue about intersectional identity in various regions of the United States and adding to the conversation pertaining to interconnected roles gender and race play in local and regional politics.

Ecocriticticism encourages readers to discover and critically investigate the intersections between collective memory, individual agency, physical environment and the notion of place. This field of study challenges us to consider the eco-psychological pragmatics that disrupts our "knowing" of spaces. I view the Heartland as a space that explores the shared notions of journeys, wilderness, and adaptation within the context of the eco-psychological landscape of the New World, particularly the American Dream—defined as life, liberty, and the pursuit of happiness. For this edited collection, the authors view the ideas associated with American Dream are interchangeable with the American Creed.

I am specifically interested in the way ethnocentric ideas associated with dominant culture disrupted notions of democracy. I and the contributors in this collection view history as multiple expressions that are collectively worked out in the context of political struggle, the conduit through with knowledge of the self and of intuitional practices are derived.[27] This book also suggests that histories are not fixed in any particular way, but that histories are a recollection of our lived experiences and an expression of communal memory. These histories don't aim to follow a chronologic paradigm, but aim to collapse time in an effort to maximize understanding and a collective awareness. This book demonstrates that there was a prior knowing, a different placement in the human idiom of constricted time.[28] This is a history that is not inherited from dominant narratives.

I open this collection with Denise Low-Weso's ethnography, "Delaware Diaspora: Memoir Of My Delaware Grandfather." I open with this piece because I am careful to attend to the intellectual examples and legacies of black women like historian Deborah Gray White. She finds that histories rooted in the body and the home allow us to resituates the histories that excluded marginalized people. I also open with this chapter because the intersection of racism and gender within the context of environmental memory begins in the girlhood of the author Denise Low-Weso. Embodiment is a way of knowing and a manifestation of some of the first knowledge. Experience is a category of great epistemic import to feminism.[29] Low-Weso's grandfather sharing his individual and collective history as a Lenape/Delaware Indian with his granddaughter stimulated memory and acts of remembering that make it possible to unlock time for the purpose of looking at how one travels through time, for example, to access the past as a way to change the future in the present moment.[30] Low-Weso's autoethnography illustrates how her Delaware Indian grandfather was discriminated against and pushed from county to county as each county in Kansas tried to cultivate an exclusively white population. Historically republican and anti-slavery, Kansas, the "free state," was the first to outlaw the Klu Klux Klan (KKK) in 1925. Despite the abolitionist and anti-racist fervor, racism was so perverse that it is prominently figured in the laws and policies of the state. Low-Weso shows how narratives are disrupted when racialized violence are inflicted on members of the community. Low-Weso's ethnography illustrates that territorial claims and citizenship claims work hand in hand.[31]

In chapter 2 "From Mexican to Mexican American in Kansas City, 1914–1940," Valerie Mendoza illustrates how Latina communities help to shape notions of home in the Heartland. Mendoza's research shows how a transnational Mexican culture evolved from the early years of migration despite the fear of loosing "home" in terms of Mexican nationalism and facing racialized discrimination in the Heartland. She expands upon ideas of new paradise and home in Mexican American memory. Largely due to racial discrimination, Mexican Americans lacked a host immigrant community during the 1920s. And although the specific Mexican American population in Kansas City that Mendoza refers to was eager to assimilate into the dominant American narratives that affirmed patriarchal gender and racial discrimination, she illustrates how important the domestic space and women's communities were in helping to establish this particular a Mexican American community. Although many were excluded from agencies and community that fostered Anglo American assimilation, the colonias cultivate permanency and stability in Kansas City during the 1920s. They stimulated the practice and observance of Mexican traditions that created an atmosphere of comfort that in turn helped to create permanent communities. The space and ethnic community was a new home, if not paradise, with a shared heritage fostered pride in self and in the group. Mendoza's research expands historical knowledge of Mexican American identity that tends to focus on Latina communities from border states such as Arizona and California and their relationships with American political ideologies such as grass roots organizing. Kansas City, Missouri was an environment often hostile to Mexican immigrants that were geographically distanced from Mexico's national borders.

Chapter 3 continues to explore intersectional identity. In Tammy Kernodle's essay "Singing and Swinging in the Heartland: Black Women Musicians Making Music in the Midwest during the Jazz Age," we observe how intersectional identities of race and gender impact black women performers. Kernodle's essay helps us to analyze how black women operated. We observe the ways gendered communities outside of the home operated in order to secure the safety of their personhood. She opens her discussion with examination of the historical significance of black leisure activities in the Heartland. Kernodle's discussion of leisure begins with a thorough revisiting of environmental memory in the Heartland. Using states such as Missouri, Tennessee, Kansas, and Nebraska, the work explores how the extraordinary talents of these black women were expressed in the leisure industries of the Heartland. Kernodle shows the privilege associated with being a black women performer in the music and entertainment businesses. The greatest example of privilege is being able to forge new public identities of respectability within black cultural communities and dominant culture. She shows how Julia Lee and Mary Lou Williams were able to cultivate lives that extended beyond the notions of respectability and liberated them from the dangerous and dehumanizing conditions of domestic work or the agricultural life associated with a Heartland version of Jim Crow. Kernodle shows how the experiences and recordings of Julia Lee and Mary Lou Williams provide insight as to how black women instrumentalists gained geographic mobility and negotiated the threats associated with Jim Crow and Suffrage politics in the 1910s and 1920s.

Chapter 4 focuses on the ways the two party political systems, specifically the Democratic Party, influenced voted patterns and negotiated democratic rights in socialist-leaning southeast Kansas. In his research "Negotiating the Middle Border: Ambivalence and the Rhetoric of White Anti-Racism in 1920s Kansas," Jason Barrett-Fox looks specifically at the ways rhetoric of racial inferiority associated with eugenics impacted local politics and affirmed national agendas by controlling the public opinion and shaping the memory of regional spaces. His essay also explores how race and gender discrimination were used to undermine one another and democracy in order to restructure communities in the Heartland to favor the wealthiest members of society. Barrett-Fox's work is unique because it explores the intersections of Jim Crow and Suffrage in the life and professional legacy of Marcet Haldeman-Julius.

In chapter 5, architectural historian James West discusses race and space within the context of environmental memory. West in his essay

"No Place Like Home: Chicago's Black Metropolis and the Johnson Publishing Offices, 1942–1975," West uses architecture, specifically the Johnson Building in Chicago, to document the ways collected spaces are used as a public transcript to marked social progress. He shows how the Johnson building became an epicenter and symbol of black progress in the Heartland. His essay compliments the research present in Kernodle and Kwakye's essays. As Davarian Baldwin states in his book *Chicago's New Negroes: Modernity, the Great Migration and Black Urban Life*, after 1915 the terms "old" and "new" no longer referred to when you arrived to the city and came to reflect one's "relationship to the ideas about industrialized labor and leisure as expressions of respectability."[32] State Street or "The Stoll" as it was commonly known served as the center of Black Chicago. West's research affirms that new Negro movement was articulated across artistic disciplines too include music, literature and architecture. West's essay also illustrates how visual culture was not limited to traditional visual arts such as photography and visual art, but a consideration in architecture during the first half of the century.

Chapter 6, like Low-Weso's chapter, is a story of migration. In "From Vivi, With Love," Kwakye charts the Heartland Migration of Vivi South. More specifically, the chapter charts how Vivi South's relationship with her grandmother, Nan Lee, helped her to maintain ideas of home. The research analyzes fifteen years of letters using methods familiar with ethnography. The chapter charts Vivi's departure from Mississippi to Chicago at seven years old to live with her great aunt and uncle. This chapter not only charts the tensions associated with establishing new utopias and shaping notions of home; this research is a story of relocation and the experience of the Great Migration. It allows readers to better understand the impact of geography and space on identity markers such as race, class, and sexuality through the lens of black girlhood.

The chapters in this collection will demonstrate the ways individuals and communities that shared a collective identity came to know the Heartland space through the lenses of environmental memory. In kind, we will come to realize how the Heartland space was negotiated, embracing both the American Creed and eugenic public campaigns. Many of the essays will also explore how gender and political movements such as the Suffragist Movement generated tensions and continues to influence the ways Heartland is remembered. In this book, we are speaking of our own volition and out of our commitment to justice, to the revolutionary struggle to end domination.[33] Another part of that challenge derives from the hierarchies that are insinuated within our knowledge-making project and in the geographies we have rendered inconsequential to them.[34] My hope is that these essays bring an awareness of place that is interlocking without conflating national histories and dominant narratives above these embodied histories.

NOTES

1. Lawrence Buell, *The future of environmental criticism: Environmental crisis and literary imagination,* vol. 52, (Indiana: John Wiley & Sons, 2009), 63.
2. Edward W. Said, "Invention, memory, and place," *Critical inquiry* (2000): 177.
3. Said, "Invention," 95.
4. Samuel P. Huntington, *American Politics: The Promise of Disharmony,* (Cambridge, Massachusetts: Harvard University Press, 1981), 14.
5. Buell, *Environmental Criticism,* 71.
6. University of California Television. "Environmental Memory," *YouTube* video. 59:51, October 23, 2008. http://www.youtube.com/watch?v=nW8D49VQB8Q.
7. Buell, *Environmental Criticism,* 69.
8. Matthew W. Wilson and Sarah Elwood "Capturing," in *The SAGE Handbook of Human Geography,* ed. Noel Castree et al.(California, Sage Publications, 2014), 231.
9. Edward W. Said, *Orientalism,* (New York: Vintage Books, 1978), "Imagined geography" or "imaginative geography" are philosophical terms that are useful for analyzing and critiquing spaces. It challenges scholars to consider what narratives associated with space are limited to the perspectives of colonizers and dominant cultural constructions of knowledge that are often constructed in binary terms associated with Western thought, good and evil, self and other and ect.
10. M. Jacqui Alexander, *Pedagogies of Crossing: Meditations on Feminism, Sexual Politics, Memory, and the Sacred* (North Carolina and London: Duke University Press, 2005), 325.
11. Roderick Nash, *Wilderness and the American Mind* (New Haven, CT: Yale University Press, 2001), xii.
12. Popular Sovereignty is a political ideology introduced by Lewis Cass. It suggested that the people of U.S. territories themselves would decide whether or not slavery would be permitted within the territory. In 1848 when popular sovereignty was introduced it seemed to reflect the democratic philosophies of the nation.
13. Robert Sutton, *Heartland Utopias* (Illinois: Northern Illinois University Press, 2009), 1.
14. Robert S. Fogarty, *All Things New: American Communes and Utopian Movements, 1860–1914.* (Maryland: Lexington Books, 2003), 19.
15. Alexander, *Pedagogies of Crossing,* 325.
16. "Teddy Roosevelt's New Nationalism," accessed July 10, 2015, http://www.heritage.org/initiatives/first-principles/primary-sources/teddy-roosevelts-new-nationalism.
17. "New Nationalism."
18. Herbert David Croly and Gordon W. Kirk, *The Promise of American Life* (Michigan: Michigan State University Press, 1914). Herbert Croly's *The Promise of American Life* was deemed the Progressive-Era's bible. Many embraced his ideas and modeled their behavior to express the values of Croly's book.
19. Roosevelt, Theodore. 1910. "New Nationalism."
20. Robert P. Sutton, *Heartland Utopias,* (Illinois: Northern Illinois University Press, 2009), 4.
21. Nell I. Painter, *Exodusters: Black Migration to Kansas After Reconstruction* (New York: Knopf, 1976), 119.
22. Sutton, *Heartland Utopias,* 3.
23. Galton and other Eugenicists of the era classified white Americans in binary standards of "old" and "new." Old white Americans were referred to as "Native" Americans. These designated "Native" Americans were believed to be descendants of the Puritans and European colonists of the seventeenth century.
24. Francis Galton, "Eugenics: Its Definition, Scope, and Aims," *The American Journal of Sociology,* 10, no. 1 (1904): 1.
25. Painter, *Exodusters.* (New York: Knopf, 1976), 110.
26. Alexander, *Pedagogies of Crossing,* 277.

27. Alexander, *Pedagogies of Crossing*, 118.
28. Alexander, *Pedagogies of Crossing*, 293.
29. Alexander, *Pedagogies of Crossing*, 295.
30. Ruth Nicole Brown, *Hear our truths: The Creative Potential of Black Girlhood* (Illinois: University of Illinois Press, 2013), 51.
31. Alexander, *Pedagogies of Crossing*, 198.
32. Davarian L. Baldwin, "Chicago's New Negroes: Modernity, the Great Migration, and Black Urban Life," *Business History Review 82 vol. 1* (2008): 141–144.
33. Alexander, *Pedagogies of Crossing*, 137.
34. Alexander, *Pedagogies of Crossing*, 296.

ONE

Editor's Note

Claims of Memory and Space

DaMaris B. Hill

I am a womanist,[1] a type of black feminist writer and scholar, one that examines how race and gender conflate in the crossroads of American culture and literary arts. Hence, my creative writing and research engage in what Mae G. Henderson and Barbara Smith refer to as a "simultaneity of discourse."[2] Simultaneous discourses that explore race and gender oppression are ideal lenses for a historical undertaking, because they aim to acknowledge and overcome the limitations imposed by social expectations associated with internal identity (homogeneity) and the repression of internal differences (heterogeneity) in racial and gendered readings of works by black women writers.[3] I also believe that simultaneousness discourses are ideal because the complexity of intersectional oppressions, particularly those pertaining to race and gender, must be explored because race and gender oppressions are inherently linked with institutional frameworks in the United States. In kind, I believe these systems are interlocking.[4] It is at the crossroads of race and gender, subjectivity and collectivity, that my creative and intellectual power is embodied, remembered and rendered. This simultaneous discourse of race and gender is a mode of signifying in my writing and research. My creative and intellectual power is a source of inspiration for this historical project, *The Fluid Boundaries of Suffrage and Jim Crow: Staking Claims in the American Heartland*.

When I initially began to consider this book, I thought about documenting the complex ways African American women's history intersected with white women's histories and African American histories in the Midwest. In writing the book and soliciting contributors, I realized that these initial conceptions of the book reduced the complexities associated with environmental memory, particularly within the context of Suffrage and Jim Crow. I also discovered that even though black women were the most obvious victims of the intersections of Jim Crow and Suffrage, they were not isolated in this form of oppression. The research quickly revealed the ways cultural restrictions associated with race and gender negatively impacted many people that live in the Heartland of the American Midwest and Plains regions. I also discovered that there was no way to discuss the Jim Crow politics or Suffrage in the Midwest without exploring the history associated with forced displacement and in some cases genocide of Indigenous Americans that lived here, particularly the Heartland prior to frontier settlement movements initiated by greed and sanctioned by the federal government of the United States of America. In public history, this period of displacement is referred to as the Westward Expansion.

It is also important to note that this book in some ways takes up the challenges that Stephanie J. Shaw proposes in *What a Woman Ought to Be*. Similar to Shaw's work, this book attempts to understand the objective realities associated with racism and sexism. At the same time many of the essays in this book seek to distinguish the objective realities of racism and sexism from the subjective experiences of individuals that lived in a racist and sexist society.

With these ideas in mind, I chose to begin this collection with Denise Low-Weso's auto/ethnography, *Delaware Diaspora: Memoir of My Delaware Grandfather*. I open with Low-Weso's personal and indigenous lineage testimony because many womanist and feminist scholars believe that embodiment is a way of knowing and a manifestation of some first knowledge. In kind, womanists and other feminist scholars believe that experience is the way women come to know the ideologies associated with their identities; and stories are the ways we teach about these experiences.

Within a similar context, Low-Weso's auto/ethnography affirms Americanist scholar Deborah Gray White's theories. White finds that histories rooted in the body and the home allow us to resituate the histories that excluded marginalized people. The intersections of race and gender within the context of environmental memory begin for Low-Weso in girlhood: in her first memories associated with her body and in her home.

The second reason I open with Low-Weso's auto/ethnography is because it acknowledges the simultaneous discourses that refute public histories and dominant narratives. The auto/ethnography becomes a testimony of race and gender oppression associated with her collective identity as a person of Delaware tribal heritage. Low-Weso's auto/ethnography and embodied testimony illustrate that territorial claims and citizenship claims work hand in hand. Her auto/ethnography is a punctuating archive that shows readers that histories rooted in the body and the home. This fact allows us to resituate the perspectives associated with regional and national histories within personal contexts.

In Low-Weso's auto/ethnography, the reader is introduced to the ways her Delaware Indian grandfather was discriminated against and pushed from county to county as each county in Kansas tried to cultivate an exclusively white population. This chapter documents the ways white supremacy was manipulated and is remembered in marginalized communities. It also helps the reader to understand that white supremacy was achieved using many strategies. For instance, prior to 1964, some Indigenous Americans were coercively assimilated into, and African Americans were involuntarily segregated from, mainstream society. The reasons were largely strategic, because assimilating Indigenous American Indians freed up their lands for white settlement and chipped away at what the dominant culture viewed as tribal sovereignty. Meanwhile, excluding blacks from a mainstream society enlarged the pool of servile labor [to include Indigenous Americans and immigrants] during the antebellum era and therefore neutralized the competitive threat of cheap black labor after the Civil War. Each of these policies supported white supremacy in mainstream society, even though they were seemingly at odds.[5]

Another reason to open with Low-Weso's chapter is rooted in the biases associated with public histories. Often public and national histories are a reflection of propaganda associated with the dominant culture's understanding. An example is Gunlog Für's theories about the European colonists' encounters with Delaware Indians in her work *A Nation of Women: Gender and Colonial Encounters Among the Delaware Indians*. Therein, Für finds that in identifying chiefs—an imperative for European colonists bent on negotiating for land—the newcomers [European colonists] often seized upon any (male) person who appeared to command some sort of following [among the Indigenous Americans]. This meant that at times men designated as sachems [chiefs] in the historical record may instead have been war captains [and not sachems] and in turn this resulted in contradictory statements concerning the reaches of these falsely identified sachems' authority. This male war captain was a go-between, a messenger, a person balancing between two groups, using that most powerful tool—words—in the most careful manner.[6] Für also concludes that Europeans were clearly aware that the person speaking for Native populations in their meetings with foreigners was not a sachem, yet he always seems to have been a male person.[7] This inappropriate designating of male war captains or "go-betweens" as sachems and chiefs could be one of the first ways the European colonists sought to cultivate Eurocentric ideas of cultural norms associated with patriarchy and land rights in the new found Americas and hence in later interactions/negotiations with Indigenous Americans.

In an aim to correct some of the public history that continues to be popularized regarding the Heartland, I must address the revisions and omissions of plural histories that took place in the earliest documenting of the country. Low-Weso's auto/ethnography helps me to accomplish these aims because her auto/ethnography illustrates how the American Creed is often in conflict with democracy.[8] Furthermore, the auto/ethnography is a collective story that illustrates how communal values are most always in tension with individual desires.

As Low-Weso's grandfather shares the history of racial conflict in Heartland with his granddaughter, he takes a risk. The risks associated with this auto/ethnography are important keys for understanding this collection and future cultural movements in the United States. The risk is associated with the fact that men are not certain what will happen to the world they know intimately if patriarchy changes. bell hooks states that men find it easier to passively support male domination even when they know in their minds and hearts that it is wrong.[9] It is important to consider whether this act of sharing memory from grandfather to granddaughter may have been an act of revolutionary feminism. In *Feminism is for Everybody*, bell hooks defines revolutionary feminism as a type of feminism that did not want to simply alter the existing system so that women would have more rights. Revolutionary feminism wants to transform that system to being an end to patriarchy and sexism. In the same book, hooks goes on to say that revolutionary feminist consciousness-raising emphasizes the importance of learning about patriarchy as a system of domination, how it became institutionalized and how it is perpetuated and maintained.[10] It is important for us to consider whether Low's grandfather's actions were rooted in an early form of feminist consciousness associated with socialist or democratic politics or acting as an ally out of cultural his competencies as a Delaware Indian. A man from a Delaware Indian society would expect women to be empowered, treated as equal partners with men. Therefore, they collectively reject patriarchal claims to power. It is also equally important for us to consider whether or not this auto/ethnography documents a type of consciousness raising that aligns itself with feminist politics in the midst of the Suffrage and Long Civil Rights Movement, in the midst of the long struggle for social reform in this place we call America. This auto/ethnography serves as an archive and model of consciousness-raising efforts. In kind, it provides many examples about how Low-Weso's grandfather illustrated the negative impact of patriarchal politics in the Heartland and how the patriarchy was enforced using violence.

The auto/ethnography also leads me to believe that Low-Weso's grandfather valued democracy so much that he was willing risk his patriarchal benefits. His stories told of his choices and his actions affirmed revolutionary politics. His stories were consciousness raising and in-spired revolutionary thinking in his granddaughter. Low-Weso discusses how from when he started sharing of his stories, she viewed herself as a marginalized citizen that challenged the dominant culture and enacted these beliefs among her peers as they played, mimicking society. The auto/ethnography demonstrates how memory and acts of remembering are stimulated in such a way that it is possible to unlock time for the purpose of looking at how one travels through time, for example, to access the past as a way to change the future in the present moment.[11]

Considering the aforementioned, I want to take a minute to discuss my understanding of intersectionality and the community making roles of marginalized women in Indigenous cultures. Für finds that the links between female gender and life—and kinmaking rituals were strong among the Lenape and Munsee bands of Delaware Indians and the up-heavals following European settlement. Loss of homeland along the Del-aware River and New Jersey coast led to an increase in the importance of undertakings assigned to women, while other changes threatened and altered women's traditional sustenance practices.[12] In this context Low-Weso's grandfather's consciousness-raising of Dr. Denise Low-Weso is a revolutionary act that recognizes her intersectional identity as white woman who is also a Delaware Indian woman. Therefore, I consider that Low-Weso's grandfather's sharing reflected a collective consciousness that recognized that Europeans viewed Indian women's influence to be contrary to the hierarchical gendering desirable for a civilized society.[13] He may have recognized his granddaughter Low-Weso as uniquely gifted by ethnic background to take up the role on the crossroads of cultures in which she could suggest a direction for an uncertain and shattered Indian population.[14] I am sure Low-Weso's grandfather was well aware that cultural encounters could mean either conflict and war, or coexistence and peace. He may have felt that in these sensitive matters both men and women would be needed to participate.[15]

bell hooks finds that without male allies in the movement, the feminist movement and associated movements will not progress. I agree and add without anti-racist and anti-sexist allies in the struggle for space and public history, democracy cannot exist. With that said, I welcome Dr. Denise Low-Weso's grandfather's testimony and ancestral presence to this work. I also welcome other ancestors and allies that support these claims to join this struggle between democracy and public history.

NOTES

1. Alice Walker. *In Search of Our Mothers' Gardens: Womanist Prose.* (Orlando, FL: Houghton Mifflin Harcourt, 2004). A womanist is a feminist coined by the writer Alice Walker, author of *The Color Purple.* Walker finds that a womanist is a woman who loves women, sexually and/or non-sexually. A womanist is one that appreciates women's culture, women's emotional flexibility and women's strength. Walker's Womanism addresses the racist and classist aspects of white feminism and actively opposes separatist ideologies rooted in race, gender, sexuality and ect.

2. Mae G. Henderson "Speaking in Tongues: Dialogics and Dialectics and The Black Woman Writer's Literary Tradition," *Reading Black Reading Feminist: A Critical Anthology,* ed. Henry Louis Gates, Jr. (New York: Meridian, 1990), 117 . Simultaneity of Discourse is a term inspired by Barbara Smith's seminal work on black feminist criticism. This concept is meant to signify a mode of reading which examines the ways in which the perspectives of race and gender, and their interrelationships, structure the discourse of black women writers.

3. Henderson, 117.

4. Collective, Combahee River. "The Combahee river collective statement." *Home Girls: A Black Feminist Anthology,* ed. Barbara Smith. (New Brunswick, NJ: Rutgers University Press. 1983), 264-74.The belief that race and gender systems oppressions are inherently linked with institutional frameworks in the United States and are interlocking is informed by The Combahee River Collective Statement which states that "the most general statement of their politics at the present time would be that we are actively committed to struggling against racial, sexual, heterosexual, and class oppression, and see as our particular task the development of integrated analysis and practice based upon the fact that the major systems of oppression are interlocking. The synthesis of these oppressions creates the conditions of our lives."

5. Wade M. Cole. *Uncommon Schools: The Global Rise of Postsecondary Institutions for Indigenous Peoples,* (Stanford, CA: Stanford University Press, 2011), 165.

6. Gunlog Für. *A Nation of Women: Gender and Colonial Encounters Among the Delaware Indians.* University of Pennsylvania Press, 2012. vii.

7. Für vii.

8. See notes on the American Creed from the Introduction. The American Creed, rooted in the Declaration of Independence, expresses core political values that include liberty, equality, individualism, democracy and the rule of the law under the constitution.

9. bell hooks. *Feminism Is for Everybody: Passionate Politics.* (Pluto Press, 2000.) ix.

10. hooks 5 and 7.

11. Brown, Ruth Nicole. *Hear Our Truths: The Creative Potential of Black girlhood.* (Chicago: University of Illinois Press, 2013), 51.

12. Für, 23.

13. Für, 102.

14. Für 153.

15. Für, 41.

TWO

Excerpt from *Delaware Diaspora*

Memoir of My Delaware Grandfather

Denise Low-Weso

My grandfather was a mythical figure in my childhood—most often not present but when he appeared, he quietly filled the room. His silence was a carryover from respect for the power of language. For many Native people, words are physical entities, so prayer and conversation are one. N. Scott Momaday articulated this perspective: "Words are intrinsically powerful. They are magical. By means of words can one bring about physical change in the universe."[1] Voicings, carried on the breath of life, create spells, so precision is essential. The wrong description of a road can imperil a traveler. The right song can bring balance. Stating a moral stand strongly can lead to social change. Uncovering suppressed family stories can heal.

I remember how my grandfather paced his speech as he told stories, so the images imprinted deeply. Once, when I was about ten, he described masked Ku Klux Klan (known hereafter as KKK or Klan) men who rode horses through the countryside. "They caught a Negro man and rolled him in hot pine tar," he said and paused a moment as he inhaled his cigarette. This allowed me to mull over his words and create a picture in my mind. "Then they rolled him in stinking chicken feathers, with." Smoke lingered over the table, and then he said, "That's what they call tar and feathering." He paused. "You don't recover all the way after that," he said, and then he took out a deck of cards and shuffled. He dealt out a gin rummy hand in silence as I imagined harsh pitch stuck to skin. His story lasts throughout my lifetime, as I still consider that cruelty.

Years later, I understand he was telling more than an isolated anec-
dote. He was explaining his own life, the threats he experienced himself,
and this was the context for his life of unsettled wandering. With his
obvious Native heritage, he was a target, along with African Americans
and Catholics.

I have heard from African Americans the dangers they experienced
during these times. People hated by the KKK were in danger if they
walked down the wrong road or familiar roads at the wrong time. I
wonder if Grandfather himself was the victim of tar and feathering, and
this indirect story was the way he could speak about it.

Another time, he talked directly about the importance of fighting
against the KKK. As a child I hardly believed him, the story seemed so
unreal. My mother was on friendly terms with several African American
families in town, and I remember visits back and forth. I went to school
with their children. One of the founding fathers of our town was a former
slave, Edward Jones Alexander (1854–1923), who left his lifetime's earn-
ings for a city park, Camp Alexander.[2] Money talks in such business-
oriented towns, so he left a legacy of respect as well as his name. One of
the seniors of the first Emporia High School graduating class, in 1898,
was on African American, Charles Terry. His grandchildren were in my
classes.[3] I lived in the east of the state. Further west, relatives tell me Jim
Crow-style threats across Kansas were serious during the 1890s to 1940s.

So as a child, I listened to my grandfather with amazement when he
talked about the KKK. In another card game, he told me, "They held
secret meetings." Again, he took his time as he balanced his cigarette on
the ashtray, then said, "I spoke against the KKK, said they had no place in
town." He found enough like-minded people to stand with him, he said.
"We let them know they had to move on." He did not elaborate on how
this happened, but later I read how the *Emporia Gazette* editor, William
Allen White, campaigned as an Independent Party candidate for govern-
or so he could oppose the Klan. "The Klan know no politics," he said to
newspaper reporter Herbert W. Jordan, "they know no religion, and they
know no morals."[4] He spoke to one thousand five hundred people in
Cottonwood Falls, a small town near Emporia. These people made a
stand against a small minority who, nonetheless, burned a cross during
White's rally. Three cross-burners fled in the darkness, overwhelmed by
the majority.

Grandfather's story made it clear that speaking up was important.
Words were an effective weapon in the battle against mob violence.

Recently a cousin from the Kansas plains, further west, told me how
the Ku Klux Klan was remembered in family stories, as they created
divisions among neighbors. Historians document Klan membership in
Kansas during the 1920s. Even before formal organization, racism threatened the community. Kansas was the first state to declare the Klan unconstitutional, in 1925, but the law did not change hearts of forty thou-

sand Kansas Klan members. Their vigilante threat was very real for a longtime after the Klan was ruled unconstitutional.

Grandfather was a man of strong convictions. In the small Kansas town of El Dorado, east of Wichita, he owned a car repair business. Newspaper reports confirm that the Klan did establish chapters in that town, west of my hometown of Emporia, by the 1920s.[5] Grandfather left the area for larger and more diverse towns in Kansas—Newton and Kansas City. He fought the Klan, but he also knew when to retreat.

Grandfather's stories about the KKK indicate to me how words have power. He illustrated how placement of words and their timing, including pauses, are critical skills of storytelling.

In his actions and words, my grandfather rallied against the Klan, at risk to his life. He fought ethnic violence, just decades after formal end of the Indian Wars. He also fought for organized unions in the early twentieth century, while working for Kansas City meat packing plants.

One afternoon he dealt us a game of casino, arranged his cards, and waited. After I arranged my hand, highest cards to the left, and looked up, he said, "Unions did not always exist." I considered this. My father was a union representative, and the phone rang often. Long, tense conversations followed, punctuated by my father's swear words about the rights of workers. I said nothing, expecting Grandfather to continue. "Men met in secret at night, because they feared the company men would beat them to death." This was not a history covered in school lessons. I was startled by that extreme violence. Then he continued, "We wore sacks over our heads—flour sacks with eyes cut out. That way the informants could not take our names back to the bosses." I could hardly believe he had experienced this hardship. Who would want to harm my soft-spoken grandfather?

He cleared his throat, hacked a smoker's cough, and continued, "If men lost their fingers or arms in the machinery, they were fired. If they fell asleep after long hours, they were fired." He gathered his cards as I imagined maimed fingers. He finished this history lesson with "That was plain wrong."

I watched him closely to make sure he was finished before I turned back to the cards. I was a child, but I knew this was an important story, one I was supposed to remember. Later, my mother talked about Grandfather's days in the meat packing plant. She said he would never allow the family to eat hot dogs, because he saw what putrid meat scraps went into them. My mother always insisted on fresh meat as part of our diet, cut by the butcher, a lesson she learned from her father. She turned up her nose at frankfurters we had on school picnics. I remembered Grandfather's story when reading Upton Sinclair's accounts of Chicago slaughterhouses.[6]

What Grandfather did not explain to me was how poverty was the top qualification for dangerous, low-paying jobs in the meatpacking plant.

Other mixed-race and multiethnic people still in the area tell me about their family connections to stockyards. Diane Glancy's Cherokee father worked there also, and she remembers: "He left and returned each day/ with talk of union workers vying for their lives—/who would have power and who wouldn't."[7] My grandfather was among those "vying for their lives." William Trowbridge writes about the dangers of the "sticker" job he witnessed in Omaha packinghouses:

> Hung by a hind leg, hogs scream and flail
> and bite. That knife can cut both ways. The bite
> heals slow. He kept inside his to and fro:
> Perforate and pull, step back, then up again,
> his face that Indian's on the nickel, squared
> and still, unastonished by the sudden spill.[8]

This physically difficult job, killing the hog, could result in permanent injury; the individual given this position in the poem is, like my grandfather, Indian. No one told me what exactly my grandfather did in the meatpacking plant, but the experience left long-lasting scars.

Years later, I realize Grandfather talked to me as an adult, not a simple child. Other relatives treated me as an inconsequential female that should learn conversational charm. Grandfather taught how I fit into the skein of a larger community. I had importance outside the household, and at very least, I should stand up and speak my words.

Grandfather was a lifelong Democrat despite the Lincoln Republican majority around him. He persuaded me to follow his example, because of their policies to protect the working class. "Once," he said, "a lifelong friend ran for a city office. But he was a Republican. I planned to vote for him, but when I got to the polling booth," he smiled, "I just couldn't do it." He voted the straight Democrat ticket to support worker ideology.

Also, Grandfather believed no man was worth a million dollars. No labor any man did could merit that extreme income. This quiet man who seldom spoke nonetheless articulated his values and passed them on to the entire family.

Most remarkable, perhaps, was how my father paid attention to his father-in-law's stories and changed politics from Republican to Democrat; he joined a union and became a leader; he broke with his own fundamentalist Christian father's beliefs. No one ever identified to me the profound influence Grandfather had on the family's values. He seldom interacted with our family when I was a child, as his problem with alcohol addiction became worse, or his self-medication, perhaps connected to chronic pain due to his disability. I suspect he experienced depression and historic trauma. Nonetheless, from my grandfather, our family learned to consider the welfare of the community above individual profit.

My father joined the county social welfare board and the library board. He became active in local politics, and his signature letters to the

Emporia Gazette editor, William Lindsay White, became famous as solo Democrat commentary in the Republican town. So my father, who was white not Delaware, was a good son-in-law to this maverick social activist. He spoke to me about the civil rights of all people in direct terms during the 1960s. Only much later did I learn his own father had attended early KKK rallies. He never told me this. If my Grandfather had not given him another perspective, our family beliefs may have been very different.

I remember my Delaware grandfather who suffered but did not quit. I celebrate what he accomplished in his teachings and his full life span. He influenced all his family to resist violence and discrimination. That legacy continues.

NOTES

1. Scott Momaday, *The Man Made of Words* (New York: St. Martins Griffin, 1997), 16.
2. "E. J. Alexander," in *Our Land: A History of Lyon County*, ed. Ted F. McDaniel (Kansas: Emporia State Press, 1976), and 160–161.
3. John Collier, "Blacks and Emporia," *Our Land: A History of Lyon County*, ed.Ted F. McDaniel (Kansas: Emporia State Press, 1976), 159.
4. Herbert Jordan, "A Klan Cross on Main Street Follows Speech," *Topeka Daily Capital* (Topeka, KS), Sept. 23, 1924. *Kansas Memory*, accessed June 19, 2014, www.kshs.org/p/william-allen-white-s-1924-gubernatorial-campaign/13257.
5. "Can't Stop the Ku Klux Klan," *Emporia Gazette*, July 25, 1921, Kansas Memory, www.kansasmemory.org/item/214409.
6. Upton Sinclair, *The Jungle*, (New York: Dover, 1906, Rpt. 2001).
7. Diane Glancy, *It Was Then* (Lawrence: Mammoth Publications, 2012), 14.
8. William Trowbridge, *Put This On, Please: New and Selected Poems* (Pasadena: Red Hen Press, 2014), 113.

THREE

From Mexican to Mexican-American in Kansas City, 1914–1940

Valerie Mendoza

With "the celebrations of the Sixteenth [of September] and the Cinco de Mayo, the family get togethers, the evening conversations . . . it was not easy for the Mexican images in my mind to bleach away. But over them new experiences were being laid, pleasant or interesting things the Americans did," remembered scholar Ernesto Galarza of his early days in the United States.[1] This mixture of the Mexican and the American or transference of culture is easier to witness in the Kansas City Metropolitan Area—a place beyond the U.S.—Mexico border. Prior to initial migration from Mexico in the early twentieth century, no previous Mexican community existed in the Midwest as in the Southwest, which was once a part of Mexico. In Kansas City a Mexican community had to be created from the ground up; it was a cultural construction. Culture and community became all the more important due to the transiency of the Kansas City Mexican immigrant population which was caused by both circular migration between Mexico and the United States and out migration to industrial, urban centers farther north such as Chicago and Detroit.

Whereas cities near the border clearly contained, and in some cases retained, Mexican cultural elements and were a combination of Mexico and the United States, migrants to Kansas City found a completely unknown and alien culture with no hints of home. Instead what greeted them was a rapidly growing city situated at the juncture of the Kansas and Missouri Rivers.[2] Migrants from central Mexico had traded their rural villas and ranchos surrounded by mountains and forest for this

27

bustling industrial city on the plains, and therefore, had to create "home" in this foreign land and environment.

KANSAS CITY

At the center of the country, Kansas City was literally situated at the crossroads of East and West, North and South and, as such, was a teeming railroad and cattle town in the early twentieth century.[3] Mexicans began arriving in Kansas City around 1910 due to recruitment at the border by railroad agents for the Atchison, Topeka, and Santa Fe Railway Company. Due to this recruitment of Mexican labor at the border for its operations all across the Southwest, the Atchison, Topeka, and Santa Fe Railway Company soon grew to be the largest employer of Mexicans in the region. Most of the initial Mexican settlement in Kansas City consisted of only men who composed a significant segment of the work force for the Santa Fe and Kansas City Terminal Railways, and later entered Kansas City's large packinghouse industry.[4] Settlers to Kansas City came primarily from an agricultural setting in the West Central Mexican states of Guanajuato, Jalisco, and Michoacán.[5] It was not until after the World War I years of 1917 and 1918 that appreciable numbers of women and children began to arrive from Mexico and the sex ratio began to even out.[6] This change in demographics allowed for the creation of a Mexican space in Kansas City.

Mexican migrants faced an alien environmental landscape in addition to living amongst strangers and having to negotiate a foreign language. The mountains of Mexico were gone, replaced by bluffs formed out of the river, and the outline of the forests became memories as migrants hardly ever saw any greenery, let alone forests, in their new industrial neighborhood. Instead of fresh air, the mercado (market), and the plaza, Mexicans were greeted by the noise of train whistles, the sight of smoke and soot, and the stench of cattle and hogs. Their sense of community was in flux. No longer did they cross paths with people they knew since childhood, the familiar faces of neighbors, compadres (those related through godparentship), relatives, wives, and family as they journeyed from home to field or to the town square. Yes, they had the companionship of countrymen, and in some cases brothers and friends from home, but they now lived in an isolated setting cut off from all that was familiar and encountered strangers at every turn. They also had to contend with different styles of dress, expectations of masculinity and femininity, and the American culture of consumerism and mass media.

CULTURE AND COMMUNITY

A distinct relationship exists between culture and community, particularly ethnic communities, and this can clearly be seen in Mexican Kansas City. For instance, Mexican immigrants viewed Kansas City as an extension of Mexico, and they therefore manipulated this foreign environment to fit their ideas of what was Mexican. In other words, they consciously tried to maintain a Mexican culture and identity.[7] This occurred in part because many planned to return to Mexico (although a large number of this group never did), because they practiced circular migration going back and forth between Mexico and the U.S., and because they wanted their children to be familiar with their Mexican heritage. Culture and spaces to practice culture were also created as a refuge from the harsh realities of Kansas City, which included discrimination in housing and schooling; police harassment; and low-paying, back-breaking jobs.[8]

For example, after settling in Kansas City, Mexicans continued to use religion as a form of cultural expression through the belief in and practice of Catholicism. This included participating in Catholic mass every Sunday, and in the feasts and sacraments embedded in this religious practice. Over time this evolved into something uniquely Mexican in Kansas City. Baptisms, marriages, and specific Christmas celebrations represented a few of these events. In addition, a national identity as "Mexicans" developed, as opposed to regional identities of Mexico, and was expressed in the celebration of such secular holidays as *Cinco de Mayo*.[9] All of these community and familial events helped to construct a Mexican environment in a foreign country. However, the practice of and participation in Mexican culture was colored by the immigrants' surroundings that eventually came to include aspects of American culture. Mexicans incorporated Thanksgiving and Santa Claus into their holiday practices.[10] In addition, they "shared" Mexican culture with native Kansas Citians through public celebrations (such as Mexican Independence Day) that their Kansas City neighbors could (and did) attend. All of this led to a unique culture that developed and changed over time.[11] Practice of Mexican culture in Kansas City was different from that at the U.S. Mexico border in that it had to be *created* or re-created. At the microscopic level this new Mexican American culture was extremely personal, while from a macroscopic viewpoint it was both gendered and generational. Men participated in certain activities that women did not and vice versa, or each sex was relegated to certain aspects of a particular event.[12] In addition, children and young adults more readily adopted or rejected new or known cultural experiences. Culture, therefore, was not static but contributed to a developing sense of community and identity as Mexican or Mexican American through shared experience, heritage, and experimentation.[13]

RELIGION AS CULTURE

Religion played an important role in the lives of the Mexican immigrants to Kansas City. The Catholic Church through ritual and tradition provided a constant in times of upheaval. Prior to migration, Catholicism occupied a distinct and important place in Mexican culture that revolved around the mass and church going and around traditions and sacraments such as baptisms, weddings, and funerals. Only on foreign soil did the importance of Catholicism as culture become a conscious aspect of *ethnic identity*. In fact, it became so important that immigrants worked hard to maintain its centrality in their lives.

Catholicism was one means by which Mexican immigrants could assert their cultural traditions, and it therefore became a lifeline to the memories of home. Early on immigrants sought to fulfill this aspect of their new lives by seeking out churches, and when they were excluded from them, they built their own. In this way, they took command of their religiosity and of their spirituality as so much of church activity were intertwined with their culture. Once a Mexican church was established, it became a center for religious as well as social and cultural activities.

Those who lived in the Westside neighborhood established their own church, Our Lady of Guadalupe, as early as 1915 and even obtained a Mexican priest to minister to them—the Reverend Joseph Muñoz.[14] This occurred either because the neighborhood Catholic church discriminated against the newcomers by not allowing them to worship or by relegating them to the back of the church. Rather than retreat to private worship in their homes or suffer the humiliation of discrimination, immigrants chose to take matters into their own hands. This was also due to the fact that the church stood for more than religion and fulfilled a major function in their lives.[15] The name of this new church and its Mexican priest underscored the importance of Mexico and its cultural connection to Catholicism— Our Lady of Guadalupe. Our Lady of Guadalupe served as the patroness of Mexico and was the dark-skinned Mother of the people. Mexicans in other neighborhoods did not have to wait long for their own churches either. The importance of a national church can be seen in an article *El Cosmopolita* published in 1917 describing the establishment of Our Lady of Guadalupe Church in Topeka, Kansas, over sixty miles away. Photos of the new church accompanied the article. The immigrants were so desperate for their own church and priest that after Father Muñoz left the area, many Mexicans from Kansas City traveled to Topeka to be married by the Mexican priest there rather than by a judge or American priest in Kansas City.[16]

While Mexicans celebrated all the traditional Catholic holidays such as Easter and Christmas, they also had their own special celebrations and holy days of obligation that American Catholics did not practice. A great many of these occasions occurred around the Christmas season, such as the Feast of Our Lady of Guadalupe, which is celebrated on December 12 and commemorates Her appearance to the Mexican Indian Juan Diego. Several issues of *El Cosmopolita* noted the observation of this event and remarked on the fact that it attracted many Mexicans.[17] Another tradition that related specifically to Christmas was that of *Las Posadas*, which took place the nine days prior to Christmas. This ceremony reenacts the travels of Joseph and Mary as they tried to find lodging on Christmas Eve. Celebrants walk in a procession going from door to door (predetermined, of course) in the neighborhood surrounding the church to ask for shelter and are refused systematically until finally one "innkeeper" allows the couple to stay in his "manger." This reenactment ended nightly with the procession's last stop at the home of a needy family who was given food and gifts. Afterwards the participants returned to the church for *chocolate* and *pan dulce* (hot chocolate and sweet breads) and the breaking of a *piñata* for the children.[18] The Christmas season is also a time for feasting on special foods. Mexican immigrants would make tamales, an indigenous Mexican delicacy made of cornmeal and pork, cooked in cornhusks. The preparation for this dish is time consuming so families would often hold "tamale parties" where female family members and friends would gather together for the preparation of this Christmas fare.[19] The Feast of Our Lady of Guadalupe, *Las Posadas*, and the making of tamales illustrate how religion and culture interconnect in the Mexican case of Kansas City. Our Lady of Guadalupe was of undeniably Mexican origin and served not only as a source of cultural retention but also of pride. *Las Posadas* clearly contained elements of sociability and culture in the feasting on traditional Mexican foods afterwards and the playing of a Mexican game for the children.[20] And making tamales for Christmas feasts incorporated indigenous food from their country of origin with sociability.

The importance of Roman Catholic ritual for Mexican immigrants occurs once again at times of baptism, marriage, and death. Births and baptisms, of course, were seen as times of great joy and celebration. *El Cosmopolita* often noted the baptisms of new citizens on the pages of its newspaper such as in an article in a February 1919 issue that announced the baptism of David Carrillo, son of Jesús Carrillo and Leonor Mares de Carrillo at the Catholic church on 24th Street. The article also mentioned that the *padrinos* (godparents) of the baby were Jesús Romo and Natalia R. de Romo and that the Carrillos had a party afterward at their home on Belleview. A May issue of the newspaper noted the baptism of Josefina, daughter of señor Nemesio Carrión and his wife, who had "un gran baile" in honor of the occasion.[21] Baptisms, therefore, were a religious sacrament and a community celebration that established familial ties by the selection of the baby's *padrinos*, who served as surrogate parents and extended family members. A baptism's importance in creating family ties through godparentship, and as a form of celebration, was underscored by its notation in the newspaper. Baptisms also served as a way to welcome a new member into the Mexican American and Christian community.[22] In this manner Mexican migrants were able to maintain and celebrate Mexican tradition.

Marriages also represented times of celebration that revolved around the church and included the construction of family ties through the marriage of the bride and groom and through the choice of sponsors or *padrinos* by the couple.[23] The sponsors served as "guides" or roles models for the married life of the couple and were also treated as godparents and family members. The wedding celebration itself did not end with the church service, but went on to include large parties at which the entire neighborhood enjoyed food, drink, and dancing in honor of the newlyweds. The food preparation alone often took female family members several weeks to complete and represents one way in which culture was gendered.[24] During this time, female family members gathered to share gossip as well as speculate about the future of the couple so that, in addition to gendered work, they also made food preparation for weddings a female social event.[25]

Death is another part of the life cycle that has special religious and cultural meaning.[26] For example, a novena is held in honor of the deceased where friends and family members gather for nine days after the burial to say the rosary.[27] This offers a time and space for grieving and mutual comfort that encompasses notions of family and community. Many church societies were formed in order to assist immigrants with deaths and funerals, and several of these reflect a gendered character. Mexicans initiated the Sociedad Funeraria Miguel Hidalgo in order to aid their countrymen with burial arrangements and costs, and the Sociedad Mexicana de Señoras represented a strictly female version of this type of group. These women dealt with funeral arrangements, such as that of Ignacio Quiñones when he died in 1915, and prayed for the souls of the deceased and the well-being of those who had suffered a loss.[28]

In addition to serving the spiritual and cultural needs of the Mexican immigrants, the Catholic Church also filled the educational needs of their children. Most churches had Sunday schools in which nuns and community members volunteered to teach children Catholic doctrine, and, in addition, Catholic churches in the various *barrios* offered elementary education to young immigrants.[29] One parochial school was started for Mexican children on the Westside by "distinguished women of the city." *El Cosmopolita* reported that these upstanding women felt that Catholic-sponsored education, as opposed to secular, was needed for the over 200 Mexican children of school age in this neighborhood. The board of directors for the fledgling school included Mrs. J. J. Grier as honorary president, Mrs. Maurice Crigget as president, Miss M. Morley secretary, and Mrs. John Dixon as treasurer. The board left the school under the direct care of Father Muñoz, and it opened on September 24, 1917, with an enrollment of twenty-five boys and twenty-nine girls.[30]

While the church served important spiritual, cultural, and educational needs for Mexican immigrants, the motives of its clergy and American layman were not always altruistic. They knew that many Protestant sects had established churches in Mexican *barrios* in order to convert the newcomers and that these groups employed charity services as a method of introducing immigrants to Protestantism. In many ways the Catholic Church was in direct competition with Protestant evangelical efforts and, therefore, tried to maintain its hold over *Mexicanos*. One scholar reported that priests tried to keep Mexicans from associating with Americans and from participating in clubs and civic groups not sponsored by the church itself. He went on to argue that this led to the social isolation of the immigrants.[31]

The Catholic hierarchy had good reason to worry as many Protestant churches sprang up in the Mexican neighborhoods in attempt to influence the newcomers away from Catholicism. These institutions included the Mexican Christian Institute, the Westside Christian Church, La Iglesia Evangelica Mexicana de Armordale, and the William Jewell Baptist Church. The Mexican Christian Institute advertised its Easter services in an April 1919 edition of *El Cosmopolita*, while the Westside Christian church ran an ad for its Christmas celebration in 1917. La Iglesia Evangelica Mexicana operated a Sunday school and offered religious worship on Wednesdays and Sundays according to its advertisement, and the William Jewell Baptist Church boasted its own Mexican minister-former *El Cosmopolita* publisher Manuel Urbina.[32] These institutions were in fierce competition with one another for Mexican souls and did as much as possible to attract this clientele. Tradition and familiarity, however, kept the Catholic Church dominant and most immigrants remained loyal to it because Catholicism served as a visible representation of their Mexican heritage.

TRANSNATIONAL CULTURE

Those who immigrated to Kansas City actively engaged in the practice of Mexican culture, yet they could not escape their American surroundings. American culture also became part of their existence and was incorporated into a Mexican American culture. A dual cultural system developed that was founded on the traditions and customs associated with their country of origin and, over time, began to include more aspects of their Kansas City present. Immigrants maintained close ties with Mexico because many still had relatives there and considered it their true home or because they periodically traveled back and forth, while others actively planned to return. They did this by keeping up with current events in Mexico, eating traditional Mexican foods, maintaining close family ties, community celebrations such as birthdays, the formation of social and cultural clubs, and acknowledging Mexican holidays such as Mexican Independence Day and Cinco de Mayo. Celebrating these cultural occasions had the effect of maintaining their roots, brought a piece of Mexico to Kansas City, and aided in the formation of community.[33] As one scholar put it, "if the goal was to retain one's ethnic identity—or assert it occasionally—then food and calendric rituals were seen as the best elements to cling to."[34] Mexicans also adopted certain American customs and holidays as their own, which facilitated a cultural exchange, the expansion of culture beyond national borders, and the regional hegemony of the Heartland. In addition, Mexicans introduced Americans to Mexico and its culture. Mexican migrants, therefore, continually restructured the meanings of life in the United States over time.[35]

Many of those who came to Kansas City at first viewed their settlement as temporary and planned to return to Mexico after earning enough money to do so.[36] Because of this belief, they closely watched events happening across the border. *El Cosmopolita*, mindful of its clientele's desire for news from home, dutifully reported the goings-on of Mexico. During its first month of publication, the newspaper gave its readership an eyeful by reporting the U.S. occupation of Vera Cruz as a belligerent act on the part of the United States. It also kept the immigrants abreast of the revolutionary situation between the competing factions of Mexican President Venustiano Carranza and his rivals Emiliano Zapata and Pancho Villa. *El Cosmopolita*'s editor supported Carranza. A fact reflected in the newspaper's pro-Carrancista articles.[37] In fact, *El Cosmopolita* printed an extra edition of the paper to announce U.S. recognition of Carranza as official leader of Mexico in 1915.[38] News of Mexico dominated the front page of the paper consistently over the years from a photo of *soldaderas*, female revolutionary soldiers, to the announcement of General Pershing's 1916 invasion of Mexico. *El Cosmopolita* also advocated that its readership vote in the 1917 Mexican election for president.[39]

Staying in contact with Mexican national events carried with it a multiplicity of meanings. Not only were Kansas City immigrants up to date with the situation in Mexico as a whole, but reading news of their *patria* lessened the miles between Kansas City and the border. *Mexicanos* could feel as if they were still a part of Mexico. In addition, staying on top of current events allowed them to see Mexico in a national and international context rather than the regional or local one of their hometowns and villages. This created a sense of nationalism and identity within Kansas City that was defined in opposition to that of Americans—sometimes literally, as in the case of the occupation of Vera Cruz. In the early stages of migration men who worked in Kansas City lived a transnational existence of necessity—working in the United States but with family in Mexico. Subsequently, they were tied to two countries. Yet even after family units joined them in the North, the relationship with Mexico remained strong.[40]

Immigrants also maintained links to Mexico by generating opportunities for Mexican cultural expression. This was achieved by inviting Mexican performers on tour in the U.S. to stop in Kansas City. For example, a group of Mexican *charros* (cowboys) stayed a week in the Kansas City area and performed a rodeo at the Orpheum Theater.[41] Movies in Spanish also kept immigrants in touch with their language and culture, and several theaters in the area began to cater to this audience, such as the Victoria Theater at 505 Kansas Avenue and the Cine Patria Theater.[42] These events fostered pride throughout the community and provided a public space for Mexicans to gather in large and concentrated numbers, which helped to ease loneliness and isolation by creating a sense of "home" in this new environment. Immigrants could see for themselves that their numbers in Kansas City were in fact larger than they appeared in the context of day-to-day existence, which, in turn, facilitated a sense of unity rooted in ethnicity and national identity. Rarely did such large groups of Mexicans from all over Kansas City come together in one place. Church services or family celebrations only included those in the immediate neighborhood or family members, whereas the arrival of entertainment from Mexico was a citywide event.

Preparing and eating foods of Mexico offered other reminders of home, and stores and restaurants tried to serve the immigrants to the best of their abilities.[43] The Nat Milgram Mercantile Company on 24th Street advertised Mexican chocolate, *chorizo* (a spicy sausage used in many Mexican dishes), and pinto beans for sale. Beans, a staple of the Mexican diet, were offered at $9.90 for one hundred pounds, and the Bernardo López company advertised different types of chili peppers for sale as well as seeds for growing a variety of chili plants at four packs for thirty cents.[44] In addition to cooking their own food or growing ingredients for Mexican fare, immigrants had the option of frequenting restaurants that specialized in traditional dishes, such as the Chin Chun Chan restaurant,[45] which sold such favorites as enchiladas, tamales, and molé and competed with the Restaurant Mexicano a few doors away (owned by Felicitas O. de Martínez) whose specialties included enchiladas, tamales, and other distinct dishes. Daniel Tijerina operated a bakery that made a variety of Mexican sweet breads or *pan dulce* for the immigrant community, and Francisco Flores of Netawaka, Kansas advertised *chili verde Mexicano* for sale in *El Cosmopolita* to help spice up meals.[46] I emphasize food and eating habits because they form such a large and distinct part of culture. The cooking of traditional meals brought the tastes and smells of home into the Kansas City kitchen and provided a sense of security and comfort.[47] Because Mexican food was unknown in Kansas City before the first migrants arrived, it was not something that could be found in other parts of the city. It therefore represents one aspect of culture that Mexicans consciously recreated in a foreign setting on a daily basis—it was a constant of day-to-day existence. For example, certain family members, usually mothers or older daughters, would wake up before the rest of the household to make the day's batch of tortillas—the staple of the Mexican diet.[48]

Food was also of special importance at Mexican celebrations in honor of weddings, baptisms, birthdays, and any other occasion that warranted a family get-together. Extensive food preparation for weddings has been previously mentioned and its gendered nature noted. Another example occurred when Nicolás Jaime held a party at his home one Saturday in July that included feasting on enchiladas, chicken, tamales, and other refreshments. The event was noted in the "society" section of El Cosmopolita. That the newspaper even bothered to list the menus for such events shows the centrality of food in Mexican culture.

Food and culture also intersect with gender in that women served as primary cooks. In addition, cooking was a skill they often used for charitable and cultural functions. One example can be found when the Society of Mexican Women held a fund raising dinner in June of 1919 for forty cents a plate.[49] Women, therefore, capitalized on their traditional gender roles and turned them on their head in order to plan and execute social events in which women were the power brokers and earners in a capitalist sense.

Immigrants organized many clubs and societies in order to foster a sense of community and a friendly atmosphere, many of which were gender-specific. Both women and men had their own separate gatherings, such as female societies like the Hijas de Juárez, a patriotic group for women that formed in 1914.[50] With both men and women belonging to societies organized around patriotic, literary, and cultural events, some Mexican clubs were thus heterosocial. Literary and music festivals proved to be popular activities that promoted Mexican culture, and the first was organized in 1914 and another formed two years later known as the Armando Palacio Váldes Society.[51] The Círculo Literario y Social Mexicano was another club that promoted intellectual and social events. After its birth in the summer of 1915, its members sponsored a dinner and dance--events that became a regular part of the club's activities. The club members proved to be such a jovial group that police broke up one of their gatherings and arrested all those present for illegally selling and consuming alcohol. A judge subsequently released them after the charges proved false.[52] Other social clubs included Club Recreativo Dance Society, formed in the summer of 1919 by Nicolás Gómez and señorita Refugio López, and Club Mexicano organized in February 1916. The latter group had its own building at 217 Kansas Avenue, which they used for dances held each week and on Mexican national holidays. The building also housed a library in order to promote education. These societies served as leisure outlets and helped Mexicans cope with the harshness of life in Kansas City. For example, seventy-five persons attended the opening dance given at the Club Mexicano.[53] Immigrants actively sought out social spaces for the company of other Mexicans in celebration of their culture, which, in turn, fostered a sense of community as the sights and sound of home came alive at these club activities and dances showcasing Mexican bands.

By far the most popular societies were those that revolved around Mexican patriotism such as the Junta Patriótica, which sponsored the annual Mexican Independence Day celebrations and the Union Mexicano Benito Juárez.[54] These *mutualista* societies were important to immigrants because through them members could affirm their loyalty to and love of their country of birth.[55] One hundred and fifty people attended the first meeting of the Benito Juárez Society, for example, and this included men, women, and children. The organizational meeting was, then, more than a meeting, but rather a family event that received the endorsement of Father José Muñoz, who addressed members of the group the following week on the importance of the society.[56] This club was unlike any other, and its popularity can be measured by the fact that a weekly summary of its meetings appeared in *El Cosmopolita*. The club offered funeral benefits for its members, sponsored cultural events as fundraisers, and honored all Mexican holidays and historical events.[57]

From the beginning of settlement Mexicans sought to show patriotism to their birth country through the celebration of the Mexican national holidays of *Cinco de Mayo* and *September Sixteenth*. The former commemorated the ousting of the French army from Mexico and the latter the overthrow of Spanish rule. These holidays were very important because they proved the loyalty of the immigrants and honoring these two days brought a piece of Mexico to Kansas. They also aided in the creation of Mexican national identity.[58]

The first fiesta in Kansas City took place in 1915 in observance of Cinco de Mayo and was sponsored by the Benito Juárez *mutualista*. The festivities included speeches and music and were probably followed by a dance. That same year the organization sponsored a celebration in honor of Mexican Independence Day that lasted two days and concluded with a dance that lasted until the early hours of the next morning.[59] These holidays offered the social space necessary to foster a sense of togetherness and community. Recognizing the significance of these cultural affairs, the following year the Bernardo López company placed an ad in *El Cosmopolita* in honor of Cinco de Mayo, and the community celebrated the day in Swope Park.[60] September 16 proved to be the bigger holiday and announcements for planning festivities began as early as July.[61] One year immigrants were urged to write to *El Cosmopolita* on the topic of the importance of Mexican Independence Day, and that same year three women were chosen as queens for the day. They represented Mexico,

Spain, and the United States, which shows the syncretism taking place in the festivities that included an element of their new country. This was further fostered in the 1920s when a parade in honor of September 16 included a color guard that carried both the U.S. and Mexican flags and men who represented George Washington and Miguel Hidalgo, fathers of the United States and Mexico, respectively.[62] These events also encouraged Americans to become more familiar with Mexicans and their culture, as seen in a photo of an Independence Day fiesta in 1926 that shows a large number of non-Mexicans in the crowd of revelers listening to an all-Mexican band.[63] Indeed, one scholar has argued that such a public display of ethnic culture was not necessarily to celebrate that ethnic culture but to evoke ethnic symbols "as a way of claiming space on the American landscape and the American calendar."[64] In other words, it was a way for newcomers to move from immigrant to ethnic.

Just as Americans learned more about these newcomers through their holiday celebrations, Mexicans became more familiar with American culture in similar ways. During its first year of publication *El Cosmopolita* printed articles that explained American holidays and customs so that immigrants would be able to participate. One article discussed the origin and meaning of Thanksgiving and another explained the concept of Santa Claus.[65] The following year a July 4th celebration was planned for Mexicans that included a naturalization ceremony at a local high school. While immigrants might be willing to celebrate the birth of their newly adopted country, they were not willing to give up their Mexican citizenship, and no Mexicans were naturalized.[66]

Another American pastime that families could enjoy together was baseball. That Mexicans engaged in this new form of recreation had many meanings. For one, baseball was the all-American sport, and the fact that Mexican immigrants wholeheartedly adopted it showed that they chose to appropriate the American pastime as one of their own.[67] The competition associated with the game bolstered feelings of family and community because an afternoon outing to the ballpark could be enjoyed by everyone, and as Mexicans in other parts of Kansas and Missouri organized their own teams friendly rivalries began, promoting community spirit.[68]

Mexican involvement with baseball in Kansas City can be traced to Spring 1919 and an announcement in *El Cosmopolita* by Reverend Estill's Christian Institute. The following week the club was organized with the Reverend as its honorary president and official treasurer. Alfonso Dehesa was elected the baseball club's official president and Luis Acosta served as secretary. Those paying the two dollar membership fee included R. Lara, S. Ramirez, O. Pimentel, A. Martinez, F. Medina, and six others.[69] While the organization of this American sport among Mexican immigrants was an obvious attempt at Americanization by the Protestant Estill, the adoption of baseball by these Mexican laborers can be seen as the appropriation of this game to suit their own needs. In essence, these immigrants took baseball and redefined it as a new form of male leisure that exemplified masculinity. Mexican men, especially those with families, could now enjoy outings with their families and show pride in community. Playing baseball was also a way to claim the public space of the ballparks in Kansas City.

Mexican culture evolved from the early years of migration to reflect a permanency and stability in Kansas City during the 1920s. In fact, the importance of culture cannot be underestimated as a key factor in the formation of these Mexican neighborhoods. The practice and observance of Mexican tradition by individuals and as a group created an atmosphere of comfort and familiarity that laid the foundation for permanent communities that included churches in which immigrants worshipped and celebrated, mutualistas and clubs which offered comfort to countrymen in times of need, and the observation of Mexican national holidays. Shared heritage fostered pride in self and in the group in an environment often hostile to these immigrants. All of which was made more salient due to Kansas City's distance from the border and lack of host community.

NOTES

1. Ernesto Galarza, *Barrio Boy* (New York: Ballantine Books, 1971), 238.
2. Between 1910 and 1920 the population of metropolitan area of Kansas City which included both Kansas City, Kansas, and Kansas City, Missouri, increased by over thirty percent from 248,381 in 1920 to 324,410 in 1920. This percent increase was more than double the 14.9 percent increase of the United States population as a whole during this same time period. These numbers are all the more extraordinary considering Kansas City's small foreign-born population—the increase was not due to immigrants settling in Kansas City. Roy Ellis, *A Civic History of Kansas City, Missouri* (Springfield, MO: Elkins-Swyers Company, 1930), 36.
3. Kansas City contained ten rail lines in 1925; it was a primary center of trade in livestock, feed cattle, and hogs as well as a primary winter wheat market; Kansas City ranked second as a meat-packing center and was strategically located as a receiving and distributing center from fruits and vegetables. As such it was an industrial town in contrast to Tangancicuaro, which was an agricultural one. See Valerie Mendoza, "The Creation of a Mexican Immigrant Community in Kansas City, 1890–1930," PhD dissertation, University of California, Berkeley, 1997, chapter 1; Ellis, *A Civic History*, 48; Polk's *Kansas City, Kansas Directory 1925* (Kansas City, MO: Gate City Directory Company, 1925); Polk's *Kansas City, Kansas City Directory volume 1929* (Kansas City, MO: Gate City Directory Company, 1929).
4. At the time, Kansas City was home to one of the nation's largest packinghouse complexes and rivaled that of Chicago. Companies included Armour Meatpacking Company, Cudahy Meatpacking Company, Swift and Company, Morris Company, and Wilson and Company. Kansas State Census, Wyandotte County, Kansas, 1915;

Bureau of Commerce, 14th Census of the United States, Wyandotte County, Kansas and Jackson County, Missouri, 1920.

5. According to historian Judith Fincher Laird, Mexicans who settled in the Argentine neighborhood of Kansas City were primarily from Tangancícuaro, Michoacan. Judith Laird, "Argentine, Kansas: the Evolution of a Mexican-American Community, 1905–1940" (PhD dissertation: University of Kansas, 1975).

6. U.S. Census Bureau, Wyandotte County, Kansas and Jackson County, Missouri. Issued 1920.

7. They did this as opposed to trying to assimilate into a community that did not welcome their presence.

8. See Mendoza, "Creation of a Mexican Immigrant Community" and Mendoza, "Policing Gender: Mexicans and the American Legal System, the Case of Kansas City, 1910–1940," forthcoming.

9. See George Sánchez, *Becoming Mexican American: Ethnicity, Culture, and Identity in Chicano Los Angeles, 1900–1945* (Oxford: Oxford University Press, 1993). In his introduction Sánchez offers an explanation of regional identities that existed throughout Mexico and argues that it was not until the revolution that a collective Mexican identity was formed; see also Robert Orsi, *Madonna of 115th Street: Faith and Community in Italian Harlem, 1880–1940* (New Haven, CT: Yale University Press, 1985), especially chapter 7. Gabriela Arredondo discusses the development of a Mexican identity in Chicago during this time period as well. See Gabriela Arredondo, *Mexican Chicago: Race, Identity, and Nation, 1916–1939*, (Urbana: University of Illinois Press, 2008).

10. Michael Innis-Jimenez, *Steel Barrio: the Great Mexican Migration to South Chicago, 1915–1940* (New York: New York University Press, 2013), 7. Michael Innis-Jimenez argues in *Steel Barrio* that Mexican immigrants to Chicago during the interwar period used their surroundings in order to survive.

11. At the U.S. Mexico border, in places such as Texas and California, one could find established Mexican celebrations such as Mexican Independence Day or attend mass at churches populated by other Mexicans. In Kansas City these spaces have to be carved out and required conscious effort to be celebrated.

12. For example, at Thanksgiving women labor for days in order to prepare an elaborate, traditional meal. Yet at mealtime, it is the male head of the household who presides over the ritual by sitting at the head of the table, carving the turkey, and signaling that everyone may eat. Elizabeth Pleck, "Family, Feast, and Football," *Celebrating the Family: Ethnicity, Consumer Culture, and Family Rituals* (Cambridge, MA: Harvard University Press, 2000), 24–25.

13. Eric Hobsbawm has referred to this as invented tradition, which he defines as a social construction created due to a need for a connection with the past. Eric Hobsbawn, "The Invention of Tradition" in *The Invention of Tradition*, eds. Eric Hobsbawm and Terrence Ranger (Cambridge, UK: Cambridge University Press, 1983) and Pleck, *Celebrating the Family*, 6.

14. Mexican migrants to Kansas City lived in three distinct neighborhoods. One was known as the Westside, which was on the Missouri side of the border and housed immigrants who worked for the railroad. Railroad workers also lived in the Argentine neighborhood on the Kansas side of the city, and the Armourdale section of town housed those who worked for the packinghouses, also on the Kansas side of the city. See Mendoza, "Creation of a Mexican Immigrant Community" and Laird, "Argentine, Kansas."

15. 1915 Kansas City Directory. Discrimination by American Catholics was not uncommon and occurred in many cities throughout Kansas. See Cynthia Mines, "Riding the Rails to Kansas" (PhD dis, University of Kansas, 1980), 1–92.

16. *El Cosmopolita*, July 7, 1917. For example, Ignacio García and Antonia Herrera of Kansas City, Kansas received their marriage license on September 18, 1917 and were married three days later in Topeka. Wyandotte County, Kansas Marriage License Record 30.

17. The apparition occurred shortly after the conquest of Mexico by Spain and is significant because it is seen as a form of syncretism by many scholars. The Virgin appeared to an Indian at the same place of worship of the Aztec goddess Tonantzin. See *El Cosmopolita*, Dec. 8, 1917 and Dec. 22, 1917.

18. The Catholic Register reported the celebration of las Posadas at Our Lady of Guadalupe Church in the Westside district in 1919. Guadalupe Center Collection, Special Collections, Missouri Valley Room, Kansas City Public Library. Posadas is still celebrated in many Kansas towns to this day, albeit in a modified form.

19. This time-honored yuletide ritual is still performed by many Mexican families in Kansas today.

20. Domingo López, "La Yarda," *Fiesta Mexicana 1988: 55th Anniversary* (Topeka, Kansas: Our Lady of Guadalupe Parish, 1988), 62; *El Cosmopolita*, Dec. 22, 1917.

21. *El Cosmopolita*, Feb. 8, 1919; May 10, 1919.

22. Pleck, *Celebrating the Family*, 165.

23. According to Pleck, the wedding "incorporated a wife into her husband's family and a husband into his wife's." It was also viewed as a community event. Pleck, *Celebrating the Family*, 208–209.

24. *El Cosmopolita*, Jul. 26, 1919.

25. Pleck has made the same observation for women and food preparation at Thanksgiving. For example, "because they cooked together on Thanksgiving Day, and in the days of preparation before that, women enjoyed the female companionship in the kitchen and could display their mastery of womanly skills to each other." In addition to the work, the gossip that accompanied the food preparation allowed women to gather and disseminate information and to exercise "their power to shape reputations and draw lines between the violators of community norms." Pleck, *Celebrating the Family*, 25.

26. Death was also a time of great discrimination as many funeral homes would not serve Mexicans and they were buried in segregated sections of cemeteries.

27. Pleck argues that funerals came to represent family homecomings. Once embalming fluid was used to stave off decomposition, it allowed absent family members to return home for the funeral. *Celebrating the Family*, 187.

28. Robert Oppenheimer interview with Father Dinkle (May 1981), Kenneth Spencer Library, University of Kansas. José García, *History of Mexicans in Topeka, 1906–1966* (unpublished manuscript, Topeka Public Library), 21. *El Cosmopolita*, May 22, 1915. The novena is another tradition that is still adhered to today by the descendants of these original immigrants.

29. Catholic schools were also used as a means to segregate Mexican children from white students. For example, in nearby Topeka local businessmen raised money to help build the Catholic school in the Mexican neighborhood so that immigrant children would not attend the all white Lincoln School near their neighborhood.

30. For Sunday school see *Emporia Gazette*, (Emporia, Kansas, no. 2), Dec. 9, 1947. *El Cosmopolita*, Aug. 4, 1917 and Sept. 29, 1917. In hopes of encouraging enrollment, the women organizers of the school sponsored a picnic in early August for Mexican mothers and their children at Penn valley Park.

31. Robert Oppenheimer, "Acculturation or Assimilation: Mexican Immigrants in Kansas, 1900 to World War II," *Western Historical Quarterly* 16 (October 1985): 116 and 124.

32. *El Cosmopolita* April 19, 1919; December 22, 1917; May 31, 1919; April 26, 1919.

33. Pleck, *Celebrating the Family*, 4, 12. Plech argues that families used celebrations as a special time and as a way to assert waning ethic identity. See page 4. In addition, family events also served as "affirmations of the national [Americanizing] mission and celebrations of ethnic group identity and consciousness." See page 12.

34. Pleck, *Celebrating the Family*, 64.

35. John Gledhill, *Neoliberalism, Transnationalism, and Rural Poverty: A Case Study of Michoacán, Mexico* (Boulder: Westview Press, 1995), 202.

36. Many of those who planned to leave the U.S. for Mexico never returned to their country of origin for a variety of reasons. Therefore, while they viewed their settlement as temporary, it was actually permanent.

37. *El Cosmopolita*, Oct. 8, 1914; Oct. 15, 1914; Nov. 14, 1914. See also Michael Smith, "The Mexican Immigrant Press Beyond the Borderlands: the Case of *El Cosmopolita*, 1914–1919," *Great Plains Quarterly* no. 10 (Spring 1990).

38. *El Cosmopolita*, Oct. 11, 1915.

39. *El Cosmopolita*, Jan. 8, 1916; Jun. 24, 1916; Jan. 13, 1917.

40. Gledhill, *Neoliberalism*, 199. In addition, news from the homeland helped to shape the ethnic identity of the immigrants in the United States. Pleck, *Celebrating the Family*, 131.

41. *El Cosmopolita*, Nov. 6, 1915.

42. *El Cosmopolita*, Jul. 26, 1919; Aug. 2, 1919; May 25, 1918.

43. Pleck argues that "many Americans defined ethnicity in terms of family origins, hardships faced, obstacles overcome—and food." Pleck, *Celebrating the Family*, 64.

44. *El Cosmopolita*, Feb. 8, 1919; Jul. 29, 1916; Apr. 22, 1916.

45. While the name of this restaurant might connote Asian food, it served Mexican food to a Mexican clientele.

46. *El Cosmopolita*, Aug. 30, 1919; Feb. 22, 1919; Mar. 1, 1919; Aug. 26, 1916.

47. According to Pleck, "the act of using a mother's or grandmother's recipe was a way for women to make a powerful, loving connection with the dead," or in this case, the homeland. Pleck, *Celebrating the Family*, 25.

48. While cooking was normally gendered female, my aunts recalled my paternal grandfather cooking tortillas for the family in the early morning hours before he left for work during the 1950s and 1960s. Nicolas Jaime Interview with the author, April 2014.

49. *El Cosmopolita*, Jun. 7, 1919.

50. See chapter 3 and also *El Cosmopolita*, Dec. 26, 1914.

51. *El Cosmopolita*, Nov. 7, 1914; Nov. 14, 1914; Sept. 30, 1916.

52. *El Cosmopolita*, Jul. 17, 1915; Aug. 21, 1915.

53. *El Cosmopolita*, Jun. 21, 1919; Feb. 26, 1916; Mar. 4, 1916.

54. *El Cosmopolita*, Sept. 8, 1917; Oct. 1, 1914. Benito Juarez was a former president of Mexico.

55. Mutualistas were mutual aid societies that were based on membership from the local community. They each had their own theme. Some supported cultural events and others provided monetary aid or comfort to community members.

56. *El Cosmopolita*, Oct. 1, 1914; Oct. 8, 1914.

57. As a fundraiser for its funeral fund the society sponsored the appearance of singer señora Luz Amelia de Cerdio of Vera Cruz, Mexico and charged fifty cents admission, and the society annually celebrated the death of its namesake. See *El Cosmopolita*, Apr. 3, 1915; May 29, 1915; Jun. 5, 1915; and Jul. 24, 1915.

58. In a discussion of the celebration of Chinese New Year, Pleck argues that because the Chinese in the United States were segregated and discriminated, they turned to their own holidays "as a source of solace and as a means of preserving their cultural ties to their family and China." This argument can be used for other ethnic groups and national holidays that they celebrated. *Celebrating the Family*, 122.

59. *El Cosmopolita*, May 1, 1915; May 15, 1915; Sept. 18, 1915.

60. *El Cosmopolita*, May 6, 1916. Swope Park was and is the largest public park in Kansas City. Having a Mexican celebration there asserted their immigrant culture in a Kansas City public space.

61. *El Cosmopolita*, Jul. 29, 1916; Jul. 26, 1919.

62. *El Cosmopolita*, Aug. 25, 1917; Sept. 22, 1917. Guadalupe Center Collection, clipping from *Kansas City Times* (Kansas City, KS) Sept. 16, 1926.

63. Guadalupe Center Collection, box 3.

64. Robert Orsi, *Thank You St. Jude: Women's Devotion to the Patron Saint of Hopeless Causes* (New Haven, CT: Yale University Press, 1996), 30.

65. *El Cosmopolita,* Nov. 28, 1914; Dec. 19, 1914.

66. *El Cosmopolita,* Jun. 26, 1915; Jul. 10, 1915. In general during this time period, Mexicans did not choose to become American citizens. Rather they maintained their Mexican citizenship, which they associated with ties to the homeland, culture, and identity. See George Sanchez, *Becoming Mexican American: ethnicity, culture, and identity in Chicano Los Angeles, 1900–1945* (New York: Oxford University Press, 1993), 5.

67. Baseball was introduced in Mexico at the turn of the century by Americans in mining towns in the larger cities, but had not yet infiltrated all areas. In all probability, those from Tangancicuaro and the other areas of Michoacan had not yet been introduced to the sport prior to their arrival in the U.S. See William Beezley, *Judas at the Jockey Club: and Other Episodes of Porfirian Mexico* (Lincoln: University of Nebraska Press, 1987). Michael Innis-Jimenez also discusses the importance of baseball to the formation of the Mexican community in South Chicago. See Michael Innis-Jiminez, *Steel Barrio.* Jose Alamillo also discusses baseball as a leisure space and site of resistance for Mexican citrus workers in a company town in southern California. See Jose Alamillo, *Making Lemonade Out of Lemons: Mexican American Labor and Leisure in a California Town, 1880–1960* (Urbana: University of Illinois Press, 2006), ch. 5.

68. See, for example, *El Cosmopolita,* June 7, 1919.

69. *El Cosmopolita,* Mar. 15, 1919; Mar. 22, 1919.

FOUR

Singing and Swinging in the Heartland

Black Women Musicians Making Music in the Midwest during the Jazz Age

Tammy L. Kernodle

The Great Migration coupled with the emergence of segregated, largely autonomous black communities some of cities of Chicago, Memphis and Kansas City precipitated the emergence of burgeoning leisure industries that not only serviced their black constituents, but also became points of social migration, observation and interaction for whites as well. Jazz pianist Mary Lou Williams "found Kansas City to be a heavenly city—music everywhere in the Negro section of town, and fifty-nine or more cabarets rocking on Twelfth and Eighteenth Streets"[1] This leisure industry, which included the common attributes of the "sporting life"—gambling house, saloons and brothels—also extended to amusement parks, theaters and dancehalls many of which, before 1926, were black-owned. From the period of 1915 until the late 1920s, black entrepreneurs in the urban cities built, defined and controlled an infrastructure that sustained this once racially marginalized leisure industry and helped mediate black popular music culture to the masses in the years preceding and following World War I. This industry would also provide "new" and "old" settlers in these cities with alternative forms of labor to the common industrial and domestic offerings.

Additionally, this black leisure industry also fueled notions of upward mobility that advanced in the post-World War I years through the New

Negro Movement and provided new opportunities for economic and social autonomy, especially for young black women. While the stories of
black men assailing the economic constraints of industrial and agricultural labor through this leisure industry have been explored through the
biographies of Louis Armstrong, Jelly Roll Morton and others, we have
yet to fully understand how black women navigated and maintained
sustained success through these industries. Several scholars have discussed how female vocalists such as Ma Rainey, Ida Cox, Bessie Smith
and others effectively traversed the nation through the TOBA (Theater
Owners Booking Association) and sparked the vaudeville blues craze of
the 1920s.[2] But what of women who never reached the national stages of
prominence during this period? What about the women instrumentalists
who for various reasons decided to remain in these regional music centers and became identified as important cultural markers of the musical
life in the Heartland? What social and cultural phenomenon allowed
these women to navigate the terrain of the Heartland fluidly with and
without threat of physical harm? Some scholars have raised and investigated such questions; they are evidenced in the biographical work and
documented experiences of Lil Hardin Armstrong in Chicago's early jazz
scene, Lovie Austin, whose work in the Chicago-based studios of Paramount Records lives on through the race records from the 1920s and
1930s, and the life and music of blues guitarists and innovator Memphis
Minnie.[3]

Extant race record catalogs of OKeh, Paramount, Black Swan, Gennett,
and others reveal an active cache of black women singers and instrumentalists who contributed to the black leisure industries of Chicago, Kansas
City, Memphis, and surrounding areas. This research seeks to further this
work through an exploration the role of black women instrumentalists in
advancement of the black leisure industry as a means of understanding
the migratory patterns and contexts of black women's labor in the Heartland considering the ideologies of Suffrage and Jim Crow. While this
author realizes that this arduous task cannot be undertaken fully in this
chapter, this work seeks to explore this topic by considering the experiences of two black women instrumentalists who worked the leisure industry that shaped Kansas City and the Southwestern jazz scene—pianists Julia Lee (1902-1958) and Mary Lou Williams (1910-1981). The experiences of Lee and Williams working the Southwestern jazz circuit during
the 1920s can provide some understanding of the varied social and domestic contexts that allowed black women instrumentalists to navigate
the male-centered spaces that governed the performance aesthetic and
the music that framed the recreational lives of blacks in this region. This
chapter will also discuss how the developing infrastructure of the black
leisure industry in Kansas City and the surrounding area provided the
means for black women instrumentalists, specifically pianists to engage
proactively in the new forms of labor available to black women that

centered around leisure. It will also explore how the extraordinary talents of these women provided them with the means to create new public identities of respectability for black women that extended beyond the commonly held notions regarding black women's respectability and liberated them from the dehumanizing conditions of domestic and agricultural life in Jim Crow influenced Heartland. Lee and Williams professional expectations also provided unprecedented possibilities for mobility. The chapter will conclude by considering how the recollections of Williams, during the 1950s formed some of the first female-centered perspectives of early jazz culture in pre-Depression era America.

BIRTH OF A NATION: CREATING BLACK LEISURE AND MUSICAL CENTERS IN THE HEARTLAND

The black leisure industry was created outside of the cityscape of Kansas City, Memphis, and Chicago during the late teens and early 1920s came to represent a shifting relationship between black folk, urban space, and the concepts of leisure in the early twentieth century. While leisure is a concept advanced heavily in relation to white recreational practices following World War II, black recreational practices in the decades following Reconstruction indicate that this concept was an essential part of the everyday lives of blacks in the Mississippi Delta, Midwest, and Southwest regions. In reference to the geographic region of the Heartland, three cities frame the most contemporary context of the culture of black leisure and the industry it spawned—Memphis, Chicago, and Kansas City. Memphis began as a Chickasaw Indian enclave before becoming the first major riverboat port north of New Orleans. It served as one of the central trading centers in the region prior to the Civil War and was the largest inland cotton-trading center in the world with nearly a half a million bales being exported from the city yearly.[4] African slaves transported from New Orleans via the Mississippi River provided an ample workforce that helped maintain the multi-million dollar economy of the city. As the city's place in the cotton trade grew, so did the black population. By 1890, 50 percent of the population of the region was black and in time their culture, music and beliefs defined much of the milieu of the city. Beale Street became the artery of the black community and was lined with boarding houses, brothels, saloons, and various businesses that serviced the needs of black migrants. It also served as the nexus of musical activity that was only probably rivaled by New Orleans in terms of diversity. The fiddling and banjo playing of country folks were exploited, as were the traditions of black laborers and showmen.[5] Black hymnody and spiritual songs traditions existed in congruence with ragtime, brass bands, string bands, and rural bluesmen and women. Memphis served also as the home of W. C. Handy, whose mass mediation of his interpretations of the blues culture through printed scores, helped create a vaudeville blues tradition that would proliferated on stages across the country. In addition to ragtime, Handy's vaudeville blues would serve as the first forms of Negro entertainment music to crossover to white audiences.

Chicago emerged as a center of commerce and trade in the late seventeenth century through its access to traffic on the Great Lakes and its spatial relationship with the Mississippi River. Later its importance in linking the South, East and West through railroad routes made it an important point of migration. By 1900 the city boasted the type of ethnic diversity that eluded many of its Midwestern counterparts and its established black community meant that the city served as an incubator for both entrepreneurial and cultural activity. A delineated class structure that consisted of the upper class "old settlers" and working class migrants or "new settlers" defined Chicago's black community. While initially diametrically opposed in their readings and understandings of respectability and upward mobility, the two merged in response to the burgeoning populations of Black migrants arriving to the city during the 1910s. As Davarian Baldwin states in his book *Chicago's New Negroes: Modernity, the Great Migration and Black Urban* Life, after 1915 the terms "old" and "new" no longer referred to when you arrived to the city and came to reflect one's "relationship to the ideas about industrialized labor and leisure as expressions of respectability."[6] State Street or "The Stoll" as it was commonly known served as the center of Black Chicago. It also represented the confluence of these ideologies and cultural identities. By cultural identities I am referring to the variant forms of musical culture, religious beliefs and traditions that intersected in Chicago's black community. Art music, Gospel, variants forms of blues culture as well as jazz proliferated and became emblematic of Chicago's black leisure culture. Black entrepreneurship also advanced as evidence in the "black and tan" clubs first introduced by the boxer Jack Johnson, theaters such as the Pekin, the first black-owned theater in the country, music publishing houses such as those of Roberta Martin and Lillian Bowes that helped popularized gospel music, satellite offices for record companies such as Black Swan, the first black owned record company and black newspapers such as the *Chicago Defender* and the *Chicago Whip*, both of which became important in the proliferation of the race record market.[7] All of these became tantamount to Chicago's black leisure industry. While many aspects of Kansas City's black leisure culture mirrored what had developed in Chicago and Memphis, the most evident difference was its cultural significance in the larger Southwestern jazz scene.

Jazz scholars have contended for years that in the years following closing of the red light district of New Orleans in 1917, major cities throughout the country, especially Midwestern cities like Kansas City, Missouri, and Chicago, Illinois, opened their doors to these musicians and that this "opening" was the impetus for the proliferation of jazz culture during the 1920s. While some aspects of this historiography are true, they do not account for the representations of jazz culture in the Southwest that predate the closing of Storyville in New Orleans. The Southwestern jazz scene can easily trace its beginnings in the ragtime craze of the 1890s, when itinerant pianists who called themselves "Professors" moved along the western most points of the musical region into Kansas and Missouri. At the turn of the century ragtime continued to proliferate as it was co-opted into concert band traditions and served as a foundational part of the popular dance culture of the time. As composers, bandleaders and musicians continued to shape the music new variants emerged. But what is clear from the scholarship is that this music, which by the 1920s was being called jazz, shaped the leisure experiences of whites and black residing in the geographic boundaries of the Southwestern region. The region spanned parts of the Heartland including Kansas, Missouri, Oklahoma, Texas, Minnesota, Iowa, and the Dakotas. As a result these states were carved into territories, which dance orchestras or territory bands would work. Each band would have a city that served as home base and then they would tour the surrounding area.

By the early 1920s, there were well over a hundred bands that worked these territories.[8] The instrumentation and approaches advanced by these groups varied. There were bands such as Gene Coy's Happy Black Aces and Ben Smith's Blue Syncopators that specialized in more rugged, earthy and unpolished performances as well as more polished, sophisticated full size orchestras like the Alphonso Trent Orchestras, Walter Page's Blues Devils and Jesse Stone's Blues Serenaders.[9] Bands played a variety of venues including amusement parks, hotels, ballrooms and roughhouses. There were even times when makeshift performance venues were created in open fields with the stage area being illuminated by automobile headlights. Diversity was not limited to the type of venues these bands worked also extended to the type of music played. Scholars Frank Driggs and Chuck Haddix describe this as follows:

> The bands deftly navigated the broad musical landscape. In the Dakotas, Nebraska, and other states in the northern leg of the territories ruled by Lawrence Welk, audiences demanded polkas, schottichses, and waltzes, refusing to dance to anything else. The roughnecks crowding the roughhouses strewn across Texas, Oklahoma, and Arkansas insisted on hoe-downs and stomp-down western style. Fans crowding the dance halls in new Orleans and Kansas City liked their music hot, preferring stomps, breakdowns, gutbucket blues and torrid jazz. Band members crafted custom arrangements for specific regions, establishing a tradition of orchestration.[10]

While bands generally worked the expanse of the territory, Kansas City became a favored spot on the circuit. Its extravagant nightlife as well as well-paying jobs positioned it to be the "capital" of the Southwestern jazz scene.

When pianist/arranger Mary Lou Williams arrived in Kansas City, Missouri in 1928 with her husband John Williams, she found the city energized by the music and sporting life that had earned it the distinction of being the "capital" of the Southwestern jazz scene, spanning parts of Kansas, Missouri, Oklahoma, Texas, Minnesota, Iowa and the Dakotas. She had little idea that her time there would have such a dramatic impact on her development as musician and ultimately position her in the nexus of an evolving jazz milieu that would overtake the nation in the years following the Great Depression. After all she was simply accompanying her husband, saxophonist John Williams, who had recently joined one of the many territory bands that worked in the area— *T-Holder's Dark Clouds of Joy*. The band would eventually become commonly known as *Andy Kirks Twelve Clouds of Joy*. The large territory band would eventually enter popular culture through records and live performances; they produced what would become known as the Kansas City jazz style. But the musical life of Kansas City was only a snapshot of the cultural/musical revolution that had ensconced the Heartland since the advent of the Great Migration.

The Kansas City, Missouri that Williams, then only known as Mary Williams, came to in the late 1920s was a simple provincial town controlled by Tom Pendergast. He served as the boss of the Democratic Party in Kansas City from 1927 to 1938, and carved the city into segregated neighborhoods. Despite the segregation blacks managed to create their own separate, but fulfilled lives. Social clubs were a way of life and blacks owned theaters, nightclubs, ballrooms, bars and grills, as well as homes in residential areas. Saturday nights were full of card games, cabarets and dances given by social clubs, lodges and Greek-letter organizations. Sunday mornings were dedicated to worship, while afternoons were spent cheering the Kansas City's Monarchs and other teams that encompassed the Negro Baseball League, and the community was kept informed of the happenings in the city and beyond by the independent black newspaper the *Kansas City Call*.[11] For many social life in Kaycee (Kansas City, KC, and Kaycee are interchangeable) was centered on jazz and the establishments that cultivated the music, but also extended to other venues like the Lincoln Electric Park amusement park that provided other outlets for black leisure culture. The Lincoln Electric Parker was Kansas City's first black-owned amusement park and was constructed after blacks were denied access to the Electric Park. It was established at the edge of Kaycee's black community at 19th and Woodland. It featured a 700 seat theater, a dance pavilion as well as a Merry-Go-Round and Big Eli's Ferris Wheel.[12] It was emblematic of the entrepreneurial vision implemented and personal autonomy that black Kansas Citians operated under that created an expansive context of black leisure in the city. But the main artery of KC's black leisure industry was the club "district" extended from the southern boundary of Eighteenth Street to the northern boundary of Twelfth Street. In this area, six blocks square, fifty cabarets with live music existed during the peak years of Pendergast's regime. There were, however, two main clubs that cultivated the jazz nightlife in Kaycee. They were the Sunset Club on Eighteenth and Highland and the Subway Club on Eighteenth and Vine. The Sunset Club was white owned but the black manager, Piney Brown, became a mentor for jazz musicians and the establishment became one of the earliest and most popular places to jam. The Subway Club was "the" place for jam sessions. Participants in the all-night events were supplied with all the food and liquor they could ingest and out-of-town jazz musicians would not miss an opportunity to play in the many "cutting contests," which pitted the city's best pianist against each other in an effort to prove who was the most musically and technically creative, there. Outside of the Eighteenth and Vine district Kansas City was peppered with a wide array of nightclubs, which included the Boulevard Lounge, Cherry Blossom, Vanity Fair, Lone Star, Panama, Elk's Rest, and Old Kentucky Bar-B-Que. In addition to these clubs, jazz was also being played and refined in the white dance halls where black bands frequently played. The most notable were the Fairyland Park, which was on the edge of town, the Pla-Mor on Main Street, and the Roseland, which catered to white and black patrons.

The music emanating from these establishments reflected a reinterpretation of the jazz styles that were being cultivated elsewhere. Kansas City had become a depository for musicians migrating from New Orleans in route to the North (Chicago) and West (Los Angeles and San Francisco), but it also had its own cache of home-grown musicians who were important in creating new variant forms of black popular music. One of which was pianist Julia Lee, whose career started at the age of four singing in a string trio led by her father.[13] Soon afterwards she began studying piano and mastered the classic and folk-influenced ragtime styles advanced by Midwestern pianists. Although she worked private parties and special events around the city, Lee came to prominence in jazz circles playing piano and singing in the band of her brother George E. Lee. In 1919 George Lee, having returned from the war, formed a quartet that featured some of the best musicians in Kansas City. Called the George E. Lee Singing Novelty Orchestra, the aggregation played the Lyric and Lincoln Halls. Lee was known not only for his leadership of the band, but also for his soaring tenor voice, which was rumored to be heard for blocks through the open windows of Lyric Hall during summer months.[14] Lee's reputation as a bandleader was infamous as he was a taskmaster and his impetuous attitude meant that his band's personnel constantly changed. Nevertheless throughout the 1920s Lee's band was considered Bennie Moten's major rival. But it was George and his sister Julia's singing ability that distinguished the group from all other Kaycee bands. During this period no other black band in the city had comparable vocal skills and this allowed the group to do well in the famous battle of the bands that became commonplace in the region.[15] Lee's vocals as well as her aggressive, but rhythmic piano playing brought her much notoriety amongst musicians in the Southwestern scene. Because the band focused primarily performing in the variety and stage show idiom, Lee mastered a diverse and varied repertory that consisted of waltzes, schottisches, ballads and swinging blues tunes. The latter is where Lee came to prominence. When the recording industry began to express interest in the Southwestern scene, versatile performers like Lee became the focus. Although Kaycee never became home to any major labels in the race record market like Chicago, OKeh, Paramount, Brunswick, and others did mine the city for new talent.

Because it was considered "off the beaten track," the jazz style developed in Kaycee was exempted from the extra-musical agents that had shaped music in Chicago, and New York. Kansas City was geographically far enough from the two cities that the recording industry, which dictated their traditions, had no effect. Kansas City jazz expanded the instrumentation and musicality of New Orleans jazz. New Orleans jazz essentially used the cornet, clarinet, trombone, tuba, snare and bass drums, banjo and piano as the basis of its instrumentation. Kansas City musicians, however, added to this the saxophone and a new musical approach built around the improvisations of individual jazz musicians and an urbanized form of the country blues. The three part improvised polyphonic melodic style that defined New Orleans jazz was reduced to simple repeated phrases in Kansas City jazz. These repeated phrases, also known as riffs, became the foundation for the melody, harmonies and rhythmic pattern of a composition. Once this was established, solos were added. Most sections of improvisation were based on popular songs or the twelve-bar blues. The blues was the primary musical foundation for both fast and slow numbers, and riffs were usually played between and behind solos.

It was the inherent characteristics of Kansas City's style, however, that increased its popularity. There were three major musical features that distinguished Kansas City jazz from other geographic jazz styles. First, it provided a flexible framework for big band jazz with the combination of ensemble and solo passages that called for improvisation and not written solos allowing players to push the musical boundaries of their arrangements. Second, the Kansas City style was the only style, which used unspoiled blues singers such as Julia Lee, Jimmy Rushing, and Big Joe Turner as band vocalists and integral parts of the orchestra. Lastly, it allowed and encouraged the utmost technical inventiveness and adventurousness among the players. For this reason Kansas City jazz, more than any other style, became the incubator of the musical revolution in jazz, even while its most radical innovators remained rooted in the blues.[16] Winston Holmes was significant in advancing the engagement between the recording industry and Kaycee jazz and blues musicians. He facilitated recording sessions for OKeh and Paramount before launching his Merrit label in the mid-1920s. In 1922 Holmes negotiated a recording session with blues singer Trixie Smith for OKeh records. However when the local musicians hired to accompany Smith refused to work with her, the singer was dropped from the session. Julia Lee replaced Smith in a subsequent session in June 1923 and the result was two records that became the first recordings of Kaycee jazz-"Waco Blues" and "Just Wait Until I Come."[17] OKeh never released the singles, but nevertheless Lee still garnered a place in the recorded history of Kaycee jazz for her efforts. She continued to perform with her brother until the 1930s, but one of the hallmarks of these performances were risqué songs such as "Two Old Maids in a Folding Bed" and "I've Got a Crush on the Fuller Brush Man."

When Mary Williams arrived in 1928, Lee was one of the many female pianists working the territorial band circuit. Her reputation for playing "boss piano" enabled her to circulate through spaces that were normally navigated only by the most proficient male musicians. Outside of Lil Hardin and Lovie Austin in Chicago, Lee also served as the few public representations of black female jazz musicians in the Heartland during the early 1920s. But in time Williams's name would also become synonymous with Kansas City.

Mary Williams's road to Kaycee was a circuitous one that in many ways mirrored that of Lee's, but extended beyond the region scene and reflected the co-option of Kaycee jazz traditions into the larger commercial machine that made big band jazz or Swing a cultural phenomenon during the 1930s and 1940s. Born Mary Elfrieda Scruggs in Atlanta, Georgia in 1910, the pianist's family migrated to Pittsburgh when the young girl was only five. Her interest in music had blossomed out of her mother's playing of the organ and piano, and Williams's exposure to jazz and blues via the TOBA shows she attended with her stepfather Fletcher Burley. By the time she reached puberty she had already earned the reputation of being the "Little Piano Girl of East Liberty" by sitting in with the many bands that traversed the city and working many of the rent parties through the guidance and protection of Burley.[18]

Williams entered her teen years performing with a number of troupes of the TOBA, which is where she first encountered John Williams. Known as "Bearcat" amongst musicians, John was a young saxophonist born in Memphis in 1905. He had traveled with several bands on the TOBA circuit before meeting Mary in 1924 after joining the *Hits and Bits* show. Mary was attracted to John's playing and nothing else at first. But he soon won her over with his charismatic ways. John Williams was dark in complexion with smooth skin, a tall, well-built frame and short, wavy hair. The combination of musical talent and good looks often made him popular amongst the women who frequented the theatre and tent shows,

but Williams was interested in the thin, brown-skinned girl from Pittsburgh, who pounded the piano like a 200 lb. man. After spending some
time talking about life and music, the two became a couple. The rough
nature of the road and the dwindling salaries of the tour made it necessary for members of the troupe to partner up. In the case where there
were romantic sparks, members of the troupe often coupled off into
makeshift common law marriages. The TOBA favored its headliners with
good salaries, but those below top billing were subjected to low salaries,
inadequate or no housing, cramped and makeshift dressing rooms and
poor lighting and staging. In addition, life on the road in towns and cities
where black performers were subject to the whims of whites, coupling up
insured that female performers had someone to protect them from physical and sexual violence associated with Jim Crow. In John's words:

> You had a girlfriend or your life. Two would live as cheap as one. That
> was the thing you had to do. Well, [there was] Mary and a girlfriend,
> who was a little older than her. She was looking out for Mary, because
> she was so young. Well, they lived together, but after Mary got all
> enthused about my playing—my saxophone playing and all that—we
> teamed[up]. This was my girlfriend. Well, we lived together and the
> other girl she started living with the straight man, and everybody, all
> the girls on there, they had a man to protect her. We weren't married
> we just lived [together]. That was happening at shows throughout all
> the big cities: Kansas City, Louisville, Chicago.[19]

One of the major problems performers faced with the circuit was the
cancellation of bookings without notice. Shows would sometimes be
stranded far from their home base without any notion of when their
bookings would resume. John and Mary experienced many of these setbacks over the next few years, but in 1927 the couple decided to marry
and relocated to Memphis. Following a quiet wedding ceremony, the two
settled into the vibrant musical life of Beale Street. After putting together
a band consisting of Mary and musicians from around the city, John
sought work. At first the band, called John Williams and his Blues Syncopators, settled for whatever was available in the form of work, but later
the aggregation, fueled by John's business acumen, secured not only a
regular date at the famous Pink Rose Ballroom, but also the best wages
offered to a black band in the city at that time. In later recollections Mary
stated that John was "a smooth talker and a shrewd character" and he
soon maneuvered his new combo into clubs and hotels that ordinarily
wouldn't hire black musicians and also started the musician's union.[20]
But the Williams's stint in Memphis would be short-lived. By 1928 John
had decided to accept an invitation to join Terence T. Holder's Oklaho-
ma-based band, The Dark Clouds of Joy.

   Under the leadership of Holder, The Dark Clouds of Joy had become
one of the more popular bands in the southwestern jazz scene. Initially

Mary remained in Memphis to complete the Syncopators' bookings, which exposed her to some of the perils that awaited black women performers working in Jim Crow era America. There were instances in which club owners refused to pay the band, and Mary often found herself the only member of the band willing to stand up to these "hustlers." On one occasion after playing a gig the gangster who had hired them at a nightclub outside of Memphis refused to pay the band claiming "I can get all the musicians I want. $2 a dozen." The other band members, all men, refused to argue with the man and went back to Memphis leaving Mary behind screaming "I WANT MY MONEY!" Although both the man's wife and mother warned her about his violent temper, Mary continued to protest until she was paid.[21]

In addition to playing with the group, Mary also played several solo dates, which proved to be just as dangerous. Being a young, talented and attractive black woman on the wrong side of the Mason-Dixon line was quite an experience for the pianist. Knowing that she was unfamiliar with the ways of the South, many of Mary's employers often threatened her with beatings or lynching when she didn't conform to southern customs. Having spent the majority of her life in the North, Mary often forgot the expectations of blacks in relation to segregation and found herself in precarious situations. In one instance she fell asleep on the streetcar and did not move to the back when white patrons boarded. When she awoke the streetcar was empty and the driver and threatening to harm her. Mary recounts the incident as follows:

> "One night I went to sleep on the street car. Usually when you sat in the front and it began to get crowded with whites you had to move to the back. I was sleeping so when we got out to the end of the streetcar line the conductor said, 'You're going to be hurt little girl, because you're supposed to move in the back.' I said, 'I went to sleep.' When the car made the last stop I started screaming on him and scratching him. I didn't understand this, you know."[22]

In another incident while working an establishment on the outskirts of the city Mary faced a more dangerous situation. These roadhouses, where Mary often played, were popular after hour hangouts that provided food, drink and music whether recorded or live for those wishing to dance and hear music after the closing time of regular ballrooms. While Mrs. Singleton, the owner of the roadhouse was kind, many of the patrons who frequented the establishment were not. "These people were ringing a bell and saying, 'I want this,' and telling me 'you're from the North and if you don't do as we want you to do. Yeah, we'll lynch you," recalled Mary.[23] Once she was almost kidnapped by a "fan," who came night after night to listen attentively to the petite, almond-eyed Mary. One evening the cook tipped Mary off that the man was interested in more than just her piano playing. He had offered the cook $50 to help him take her to his place in Mississippi. When she learned of the kidnapping plot, a terrified Mary ran to the restroom, locked the door, and climbed out the window. She was too frightened ever to return for her pay and later learned that the man had stayed in Memphis for two weeks trying to take Mary to Mississippi. That night she learned a lesson that would remain with her until death—that her talent did not shield her from the reality of being a black woman living in a hostile environment.

In 1928 Mary finished her engagements in Memphis and left for Oklahoma City to join her husband. The 700 plus mile trip was quite taxing for the young woman as most of the major roadways leading through the Midwest were not paved or in good condition. The pianist not only had to be concerned with being a black woman traveling across the country without male companionship, but also with the hazards that lay on the roadway. When she arrived in Oklahoma in August of 1928 Mary was surprised at how successful the band had become. The Clouds of Joy had gained status as one of the leading territorial bands in the Southwest playing mainly dance music. Although jazz was becoming quite popular throughout the region, the Clouds' repertoire emphasized romantic ballads, pop tunes, and both Viennese and popular waltzes. John, quite anxious to have his wife's talents displayed, immediately invited her to the band's next rehearsal hoping to garner her an audition with Kirk. The musicianship and showmanship of the band impressed Mary.

> John was anxious to show me off musically, for he was proud of my ability. Though out of my mind from the journey, I went without sleep to make rehearsal the next morning. Holder's boys rehearsed two days a week, beginning 11 am; and I was in the hall by nine. I don't know what Holder's band made of me, but I thought them the handsomest bunch of intellectuals I had seen so far. . . . They played jazz numbers and better commercial things. They were all reading like mad, and I had to admit it was a good and different orchestra: smooth showmanship (minus the 'Tom-ing' or comedic antics that bands often used to draw in white audiences) coupled with musical ability.[24]

It's not clear if Mary played for the band during this initial meeting, but she would often accompany them during their performances throughout Oklahoma, Texas and Missouri mending buttons, and attending to some of the domestic cares of the band members. In late 1928 after a series of financial setbacks, the band moved to Kansas City where it was booked at the Pla-Mor Ballroom. Mary, who had returned to Pittsburgh to attend the funeral of her stepfather, joined John in 1929. Although not an official part of the band, which by now had become known as Andy Kirk's Twelve Clouds of Joy, Mary would sit in occasionally stirring audiences with her boogie-woogie renditions. She spent the majority of her time taking in the nightlife of Kaycee. She frequented the many cabarets that lined the 18th and Vine district, often accompanied by two young women known only as Lucille and Louise.

Williams, like Julia Lee, avoided some of the setbacks that excluded some female musicians from navigating the spaces that enabled musicians to learn and develop. In Kaycee these spaces consisted primarily of the jam sessions or "cutting contests" that musicians held nightly. These were not simply competitions that attempted to establish the most talented musicians, although they sometimes were just that, they also served as "grassroots" musical conservatories where musicians worked out new ideas or transferred knowledge to one another. The fact that these were largely male-centered spaces meant to female musicians were not often exposed to these knowledge bases that would inevitably fuel some of the musical currents that would define the jazz performance aesthetic during the 1930s and 1940s and situate the solo as the exponent of one's musical ability. Williams's participation in many of the sessions during her years in Kaycee reveal to us how her musical abilities were read by peer male musicians. In the short time she had resided in the city, Williams soaked up the blues, boogie woogie and ragtime piano styles cultivated there as well as indigenous jazz styles that were meted out nightly in these cutting contests. All of these would become evident in her playing and arranging in the decades to come.

KAYCEE AND THE MAKINGS OF MARY LOU WILLIAMS

As a pianist Mary would greatly be influenced by the "happenings" of Kansas City's nightlife, but the Kirk band shaped her evolution into a composer and arranger and earned her an indelible place in the history of big band jazz. Through trial and error and instructional sessions with Kirk, Mary learned the basics of jazz arranging. For an hour each day Kirk came to Mary's house and she watched how he voiced his arrangements. "Andy knew that I had ideas—I was writing all along but I couldn't write it down. I'd give them ideas during the rehearsals. Maybe they wanted to play a song like 'Singing in the Rain' and I'd say, 'well, listen to this.' Andy would take it down real fast but sometime they didn't at all." After several weeks Mary decided to write her own arrangement. Although problematic, the composition showed much promise. Kirk corrected the voicings of several of the instruments and Mary began writing at a feverish pace. But the two often heard the music differently and Mary struggled to recreate the sounds she heard in her head.

> I discovered chords and Andy used to say to me, "You can't do that. It's against the rules of writing music." I said, "But I hear a sixth in this chord." He said, "But you can't do it." I said, "I'm going to do it." I did the arrangement of, before I did "Walkin'," trumpet and three saxo-

phones. We only had three saxophones and one trumpet and trombone, something like that. So what I did, I put a trumpet in and I had three saxophones to play four-part harmony. He kept telling me it was against the rules of the chord. In that year I guess it was but I was hearing—I found these things on the piano and I said, this will sound good—it sounds good here. After a while I started arranging it.[25]

These early attempts to convert notes from her head to paper were often cumbersome, but the band continued to aid Mary in her development. Mary continued to experiment with new ideas and eventually her arrangements would become the essence of Kirk's mature swing sound.[26] Her arrangements and piano playing would be key to Kirk landing his first recording sessions with Vocalion and Brunswick. During their initial audition, the regular pianist, Marion Jackson, was absent after being injured in a car accident in Topeka. Mary was called in at the last minute and her ability to play anything at any time not only helped the band gain a recording contract with Brunswick/Vocalion, but also impressed the bandleader. Kirk would later state that "no one had the wildest idea she'd be a big factor in our landing an excellent two-year recording contract, or wilder yet, that she would make jazz history."[27] Yet he retained Jackson as the band's pianist, explaining that he believed the hard life of "one-niters" would be difficult for a woman. Kirk's justification for retaining Jackson is fraught with contradiction, as he, by this time, was fully aware of Mary's touring schedule on the TOBA circuit. It is more likely that Kirk felt a certain amount of loyalty to Jackson and thought that he needed the income more than Mary, who was married to John Williams. Whatever the reason, Kirk was adamant about keeping Jackson and went forward with the recording dates.

The first recording session with Vocalion was planned for November 7, 1929, at radio station KMBV in Kansas City. Jackson did show up for the session, but was replaced by Mary when Kapp insisted that she play. Kirk would later state that "because Mary Lou made the audition I felt it only fair that she make the record date too," but sources indicated that it was the complete opposite.[28] Nevertheless Jackson was replaced by Mary and the band recorded two of Mary's compositions: "Mess-A-Stomp" and "Blues Clarinet Stomp." The next session, for Brunswick on November 11, 1929, yielded another Mary original, "Froggy Bottom," [Brunswick 01211] which had already proven to be quite popular with audiences; and a collaborative effort between Kirk and Mary called "Corky Stomp." [Brunswick 01211][29]

Although released separately, the tunes "Froggy Bottom" and "Mess-A-Stomp" proved to be quite successful in the retail market and reveal some important aspects about the ways Mary Williams worked, of her early compositional style. Both compositions are rooted in the Kansas City approach of constructing performances on short, tuneful riffs with an emphasis on laidback swing rhythms. "Mess-A-Stomp," although written as an up tempo piece, is rhythmically mired down by the band's inability to swing in a relaxed manner. Following a short introduction by the horns, and a noticeable rhythmic break, the clarinet enters with the main melody, accompanied by the horns and a rhythm section comprised of banjo, piano and tuba. While the drums are included in the ensemble they are hardly audible on the extant recordings. Another rhythmic break transitions into a banjo solo accompanied by Kirk's very noticeable tuba. The saxes enter with a short riff that leads into a trumpet solo, accompanied by clarinet, saxes and rhythm section. Williams enters with an unaccompanied piano solo that is a synthesis of the boogie woogie and stride piano styles. Mary's mastery of the stride style is prominent and she often punctuates the syncopated melodies played by the right hand with heavy left hand motives. This interaction between a strong swinging left hand and a melodically syncopated right hand became indicative of the Mary's style. The ensemble returns with a new melodic motive and the drummer, for the first time, is audible in the form of rhythmic cymbal punctuations. Following a short banjo solo, the horns and saxes exchange melodic material in a short section of call and response before the performance ends with the ensemble playing a final sustained chord and cymbal crash. There are two unifying sections of this composition: the soulful, trumpet and piano solos. The entrance of these solos alter the mood of the arrangement by transitioning it from the static rhythm of the opening section with the clarinet soloist and the ensemble to the last chorus, consisting of the call and response passages between the brass and reed sections. It is in this early arrangement that one hears Williams, whose style had been groomed in the blues she heard as a young child, the vaudeville shows of the TOBA, and the jam sessions and nightlife of Kansas City, attempting to fuse these idioms into the "sweet" band rhythms and harmonies that had defined Kirk's sound up until this point. This is the beginning of the "loosening" of the Kirk sound. The difficulty the band has in swinging the written rhythm is evidence that Williams' arrangement set rhythmic requirements that the band had not encountered in previous arrangements.

On "Froggy Bottom" the necessary rhythmic adjustments are made primarily because of the dominance of Mary's piano. The performance offers early insight into the formulation of Mary's piano style, which displays remnants of Earl Hines' approach as she consistently breaks up the "stride time" in the left hand with displaced chords and disjunct harmonies, "walking" tenths, right hand octaves, and tremolos; and her trademark style of stomping rhythmic accents in the left hand (a la Jack Howard, a Pittsburgh-based pianist). But what is most evident in these early recordings is Mary's desire to transfer the soul and emotion of the blues, boogie-woogie, and other black vernacular forms to big band arrangements. These approaches and others discussed later would position the Kirk band in the continuum between the New Orleans style of jazz, the Kansas City approaches of Benny Moten and later Count Basie and the emerging East Coast style of swing. They would earn Williams the distinction of being one of the most innovative arranger of the Swing era, and be the agent of disagreement between Mary Williams and Andy Kirk.

In the months immediately following these first sessions Kirk would successfully tour the East Coast, but he would refuse to add Willliams as a permanent member of the band. It was not until during a 1930 recording session for Brunswick, during which A and R agent Jack Kapp made it clear to Kirk that much of the band's appeal had to do with Williams that the bandleader finally relented. That session would not only feature Williams's arrangements, but also produce two solo records that would document her early piano style and mark the changing of her name. Mary recorded two original compositions, "Drag 'Em" which she described as a blues and "Night Life," an up tempo piece that highlighted her ability to improvised in the Harlem stride style during break periods from the Clouds's sessions. As a marketing ploy Kapp, rationalizing that "Mary" was too plain a name to put on the label, added "Lou" to her name. From that point until her death in 1981 Mary would be known as Mary Lou Williams. At the time she was unaware of how popular these tracks would be and never raised the question of royalties. These recordings were redistributed and included in an album of "barrelhouse piano" during the forties, but Mary was never paid. Shortly after their release Mary threaten legal action in order to stop the redistribution. Despite the interest these early recordings drew, the Clouds would not record again until 1936. They set out on a tour of one-niters and college dates across Pennsylvania, Ohio and upstate New York before once again reaching New York City late in 1930.

THE VIEW FROM MY WINDOW: THE FRAMING OF JAZZ THROUGH AUTOBIOGRAPHY

While the direct impact of the Southwestern jazz scene is heard in the arrangements and recorded solo piano performances of Mary Lou Williams from this period, the musician also left a legacy of first-hand accounts that provide an unusual perspective of early jazz culture. In 1954 Williams was tapped by the British publication *Melody Maker* to write a series of articles recounting her experiences playing with some of the major jazz musicians of the time. Williams, who had longed departed from the Kirk band was embarked on a European stint that had begun in England and also taken her to France. While European audiences had enthusiastically received her, Williams was disheartened by the working and living conditions and the exploitation she faced at the hands of British promoters. Nevertheless, the pianist had decided to write an auto-biography that would chronicle her years as a performer.

While a finished autobiography was never completed, notes from this effort were compiled and edited by Max Jones, writer for *Melody Maker*, into a compendium of eleven articles that formed a series called *Mary Lou Williams: My Life with the Kings of Jazz*.[30] Williams was clear in her intentions, she would not reveal intimate things that might damage the reputations of the musicians discussed. The result was one of the first histories of the genre told from the vantage point of a black woman. In many ways in encapsulated the histories of the black cultural industry with migration narratives and a historical trajectory of black advancement and intellectual pursuit in despite Jim Crow. In reference to Kansas City and the southwestern jazz scene, Williams' accounts historicize the vibrant and competitive nature of the jam sessions. She framed one of the most quoted accounts of a jam session that included saxophonists Coleman Hawkins, Lester Young, Ben Webster, and Herschel Evans in 1954.

> The Cherry Blossom was a new nightclub richly decorated in Japanese style even to the beautiful little brown-skinned waitress. The word went around that Hawkins was in the Cherry Blossom and within about half an hour there were Lester Young, Ben Webster, Herschel Evans, Herman Walder and one or two unknown tenors piling in the club to blow. Coleman didn't know the Kaycee tenor men were so terrific and he couldn't get himself together though he played all morning. I happened to be nodding that night, and around 4 a.m. I awoke to hear someone pecking on my screen. I opened the window on Ben Webster. He was saying "Get up pussycat. We're jamming and all the pianists are tired out now. Hawkins has got his shirt off and is still blowing. You got to come down." Sure enough when we got there Hawkins was in his singlet taking turns with the Kaycee men. It seems he had run into something he didn't expect . . . When at last he gave up, he got straight in his car and drove to St. Louis.[31]

In addition to documenting the culture of the jam sessions, Williams's article accounts also provided insight into how vital the black leisure industry of the 18th and Vine district was paramount to the economic stability of the city, and the bands that provided the musical soundtrack. In addition to the bands of Bennie Moten, Walter Page, and George Lee, Williams also speaks the names of musicians who are absent from conventional jazz histories.

CONCLUSION

In the period between 1915 and 1926, black entrepreneurs throughout the Heartland created an industry around black leisure culture that included

62 Tammy L. Kernodle

an entertainment circuit, venues, publishing houses and eventually recording companies (Black Swan) that mass mediated the music that accompanied their culture to mass audiences. As this culture became more and more integrated into the cultural milieu of the Jazz Age, whites became more aware of the financial and commercial potentials of this music and this industry. In time many of the black-owned venues that had supported the black leisure industries of Kansas City, Memphis, and Chicago closed or were over taken by whites that did not advocate for integration. The repeal of Prohibition, which had ignited some of aspects of this cultural phenomenon, as well as the Great Depression and the phenomenon of "cultural slumming" that overtook the social exchanges that took place in these spaces greatly impacted the black leisure industry in the late 1920s. Many of the spaces that had fed America's consumption for black culture became a distant memory. Throughout the 1930s Kansas City would remain the home base for Andy Kirk's band, Mary Lou and Julia Lee. Following a serious accident while traveling with the Lee Novelty Orchestra, Julia decided no longer to work the Southwestern circuit after 1934 and settled into a long-term stint at Milton's, a club opened by Milton Morris located on Troost Avenue. Milton's would become a favored destination for tourists and locals as nightly Lee served up the risqué songs that were preserved by race records. Financially her stint at Milton's provided her with a sustained living, but she also scored a number of hit records for Capitol Records during the 1940s and early 1950s. Her records were some of the top R and B vocal recordings of the time and included "Gotta Gimme Whatcha Got," which peaked at number 3 on the R and B charts in 1946 and "King Size Papa" which was number 1 for nine weeks on the R and B charts in 1948. (Yanow) When she died in 1958, she was still identified as one of the hallmarks of the Kansas City music scene and represented one of the last vestiges of the "Golden Age of Territory Bands."

The popularity of Mary Lou Williams's arrangements would lead to her producing works for famed bandleaders Jimmie Lunceford, Duke Ellington and Benny Goodman. As the big band crazed continued into the early 1940s, Williams would leave the band citing misunderstandings with male musicians who no longer valued her place in the organization, and frustrations with Kirk's business practices and set off in new musical directions as a solo pianist. She would not return to Kansas City until the late 1970s when she was honored by the city with the naming of a street in the 18th and Vine district and a performance of her jazz mass. But even until her death she would credit the city with being key to her development as a musician.

Despite the limited historical record that has been generated chronicling the role of black women instrumentalists the 1910s and 1920s, the experiences and extant accounts and recordings of Julia Lee and Mary Lou Williams help provide some insight as to how black women instrumentalists gained geographic mobility and personal autonomy through the black leisure industry that precipitated the rise of jazz and blues culture in the Heartland.

NOTES

1. Mary Lou Williams as quoted in "Mary Lou Williams: My Life with the Kings of Jazz: Mr. 5x5 had a Ten block voice." *Melody Maker* 30 (April 24, 1954): 5.

2. Daphne Duvall Harrison, *Black Pearls: Blues Queens of the 1920s* (New Jersey: Rutgers University Press, 1998), Angela Y. Davis, *Blues Legacies and Black Feminism: Gertrude "Ma" Rainey, Bessie Smith and Billie Holiday* (New York: Pantheon Books, 1998); Tammy L. Kernodle, *Soul on Soul: the Life and Music of Mary Lou Williams* (Boston: Northeastern University Press, 2004).

3. James Dickerson, *Just for a Thrill: Lil Hardin Armstrong, First Lady of Jazz* (New York: Cooper Square Press, 2002), also see Tammy Kernodle, *Soul on Soul*, Boston: Northeastern University Press, 2004.

4. Dickerson, 3.

5. Kernodle, 42.

6. Baldwin, 28.

7. Vincent, 1992.

8. Driggs and Haddix 62.

9. Driggs and Haddix, 62.

10. Driggs and Haddix, 63.

11. The Negro Baseball League was founded in Kansas City, Missouri and the games played in the city were held at Muelebach Park. The Monarchs wad the home team for Kansas City and boosted a roster that included some of the most talented black players at the time, including Satchel Page.

12. Diggs and Haddix, 30.

13. Unterbrink, 57.

14. Driggs and Haddix, 42.

15. Pearson, 148.

16. Hobsbawn, 78.

17. Driggs and Haddix, 45–46.

18. For more information on the life and music of Mary Lou Williams see Tammy L. Kernodle, *Soul on Soul: the Life and Music of Mary Lou Williams* (Boston: Northeastern University Press, 2004) and Linda Dahl, *Morning Glory A Biography of Mary Lou Williams* (New York: Pantheon 1999).

19. Kernodle, 35.

20. Wilson "Mary Lou Williams Oral History Interview."

21. Kufrin, 161.

22. Wilson "Mary Lou Williams Oral History Interview."

23. Wilson "Mary Lou Williams Oral History Interview."

24. For additional information on the history of Andy Kirk and the Clouds see Gene Fernett, "Andy Kirk and his Clouds of Joy," *Swing Out: Great Negro Dance Bands* (Midland, Michigan: The Pendell Company, 1970): 77–82.

25. Wilson "Mary Lou Williams Oral History Interview."

26. Mousouris, 81. Later Mary would increase her knowledge of music theory with the help of Don Redman, Edgar Sampson, Milton Orient and Will Bradley.

27. Kirk, 70–71.

28. Driggs and Kirk, 14.

64   *Tammy L. Kernodle*

29. Driggs and Kirk, 14.

30. The idea of writing an autobiography was something Williams revisited throughout the remainder of her life. She never fully completed one, but there are several notes and sketches housed in the Mary Lou Williams Collection at the Institute of Jazz Studies at Rutgers University in Newark.

31. Kernodle, *Soul on Soul*, 55.

FIVE

Negotiating the Middle Border

Ambivalent Rhetorics of White Anti-Racism in 1920s Kansas

Jason Barrett-Fox

Joining the union forty years after its pro-slavery neighbor to the east, Kansas represented in the middle of the nineteenth century not just a literal frontier but a political one, a middle border between, not only the east and the west but the north and the south, a space rife with the suggestive potential of a becoming nation. Solidifying its identity through bloody battles with Missouri slave traders, as the territory emerged into statehood and the country fractured, it appeared that Kansas would serve as a place of rest for African Americans, a place of peace and prosperity. But despite its proud abolitionist history, many if not most white Kansans—even abolitionists—still held on to a belief in racist biological and cultural hierarchies. As William Tuttle puts it, "[t]his conflict between lofty ideas and racist realities has been the central theme of the African American history of Kansas."[1] Making plain the middle border between ideals and reality along the axes of labor, education, and politics, this chapter elaborates the complex relationships between white anti-racists in Kansas in the 1920s, who through different means and for different reasons attempt to bring the plight of black Kansans to national attention, paving the way for the groundbreaking educational reforms borne from the state in the middle of the twentieth century.

THE KLAN IN LABOR/LABOR IN THE KLAN

The twentieth century revival of the Ku Klux Klan offered a markedly different organization than that seen during Reconstruction, different in its emphasis on the "civic" and "Christian" virtues of the white race and its (at least nominal) stance against the use of violence.[2] The character of the new Klan is often attributed to Thomas Dixon, Jr., D. W. Griffith, and William J. Simmons, the first two for repopularizing the narrative of white supremacy and the latter for reinstitutionalizing it. Griffith famously based his 1915 blockbuster *Birth of a Nation* on Dixon's book *The Clansman*, and Simmons, a defrocked Methodist minister whose "ultimate goal was to found his own fraternal society," came up with the new Klan's motto and "'dreamed up' the emblems, tokens, rituals, and regalia" of the society while bedridden after an traffic accident, eventually earning $90,000 from the copyrights.[3] Though Simmons and his recruits initiated this second phase of the Klan, its pro-American, pro-white agenda did not garner significant numbers until WWI consolidated the message of white men as leaders and defenders against "[e]nemy aliens, slackers, idlers, unpatriotic citizens, immoral women, and evildoers of every description," especially blacks—a marked and fundamentally important elision, a subtext, a dog-whistle, and a crucially foregone conclusion.[4]

Though the Klan and organized labor were initially opposed in interest, their union in Kansas was consummated in 1919 when Republican Governor Henry Allen (1919–1923) backed a law that created the Kansas Court of Industrial Relations, a sweeping piece of legislation that sharply limited the power of organized labor in Kansas.[5] The law came into being as a response to a national coal strike that virtually shut down the mining industry, throwing the mostly Republican ownership into an uncomfortable financial lurch and threatening to erase one of the most lucrative industries in the state. In a 1920 debate with Samuel Gompers, Allen made the case that "[o]rganization has become a huge thing like Frankenstein in its potentiality" that demanded regulation, though he promised that the law would "not take away from the individual workman the divine right to quit work."[6]

Despite being known as an agricultural zone, mining was big business in Southeast Kansas, even beyond coal, its primary export. Crawford County during these years was second only to Belgium in the production of zinc. While other historians have argued that Allen "was a bitter enemy of the Invisible Empire" (Jones 10), the facts suggest a different conclusion: his attempted 1927 elimination of the Klan from Kansas consisted of little more than smoke and mirrors covering a larger and ongoing political concern: union-busting, and it worked to kindle a radical pro-Klan underground presence in the state. Labor and the Klan were in sync: in the case of a 1919 railroad workers' strike, for instance, seventy percent of the workers struck and, almost without exception, the remaining thirty percent were black—excluded, based on race, from unions.[7] When *The New Republic* claimed, in Allen's favor, that "it is not sufficient to argue that the worker becomes a serf under the Kansas system," they failed to consider racial politics on the ground.[8]

When the Klan and organized labor became interwoven, Allen pushed to eliminate the former and "made it unlawful to picket for the purpose of suspending the operation" of what he deemed "'essential' industries," industries populated mainly by second generation Americans whose parents had migrated from Italy and Eastern Europe answering the call of the original mining boom in the 1880s and 1890s, many of whom where friendly with the new Klan and its Americanizing directive (Sloan 395). While popular with his constituents, the subtle perniciousness of the law came in the fact that those essential industries almost completely coincided with those in which organized labor had a strong, even dominating, presence. When his industrial court law was deemed unconstitutional by the Supreme Court in 1925, Allen moved from attacking unions specifically and went after their constituents by means of their secondary organizational structure, the Klan. "Governor Allen was [partially, at least] responsible for the support that the shop craftsmen were giving the Invisible Empire," and he aimed to work that mutual affiliation to his advantage.[9] His ostensible fight against the Klan, leading up to their overt 1927 ouster from the state, then, functioned as a clever political alibi that harkened back as a rejoinder to his failed industrial court law.

By 1924, the KKK in Kansas had grown strong. Its membership, particularly in south central and southeastern Kansas, exceeded 100,000 members, according to Crawford County's pro-Klan newspaper and the flagship of pro-Klan papers in the state, *The Independent*. That number included "4,600 in Crawford County alone;" in fact, Pittsburg, KS, the county seat of Crawford County, was an early adopter and boasted one of the very first local Klan organizations in the state.[10]

As early as 1919, it became obvious to the governor that "the Ku Klux Klan had united with labor forces," and he used this fusion to accomplish the Klan's expulsion from the state.[11] Allen proclaimed the 1927 ouster of the KKK as a great victory for human tolerance and the state of Kansas, and it was, to a degree. Kansas became the first state to legally eject the Klan from within its borders, and others followed suit. He was able to shore up his national reputation, and organized labor suffered a terrible blow. The Klan, however, used the maneuver to consolidate membership and garner prestige, if only temporarily, the rebuff serving as a negative proof of its cultural significance. As Samuel Gompers, Allen's interlocutor during the 1920 Carnegie Hall debate about the Industrial Court Law put it, "the time [was] at hand when it must be determined whether eternal principles of freedom, of justice and democracy shall hold sway or be supplanted by the tyranny and injustice as of old."[12]

A WAR OF WORDS: *THE INDEPENDENT* AND THE HALDEMAN-JULIUS PUBLISHING COMPANY

While Allen lit the rhetorical fireworks of racial equality to finish the misdirection of killing organized labor in Kansas, he ignited a radical Klan underground, newly impassioned by the structural challenge and determined to exist as an open secret. As Orin Strong, publisher of the *The Independent*, based in the Crawford county village of Mulberry, explained in 1924,

> Of course the Kansas Klan will ignore the Kansas supreme court decision and go right on to do business . . . the Kansas Klan will continue to function "just as [the] anti-slavery spirit of the North rose in keen rebellion [to the] of spirit against the Dred Scott decision."[13]

The ruling functioned as a clarion call, as proof of the organization's legitimacy and cultural power, of its institutional fluidity and social necessity.

Strong's 1924 appointment to the editorship of *The Independent* by new owner and head of the Mulberry Klan J. F. Shortridge represented a turning point in the paper's history. That year, the paper's editorial staff decided to embrace the demographic layout of Crawford County by soliciting the readership of laborers.[14] That year, the paper initiated numerous new columns taken from such periodicals as *The Illinois Miner* and brought together its strong pro-Klan message and an emergent focus on labor. This was a particularly ingenious strategy, as labor (not the Klan) had been significantly weakened by four years under Allen's industrial court law, which would not be repealed until the next year. The Klan, which needed membership, saw organized labor as a possible well to tap for financial support and sought to consolidate the children of immigrants affiliated with mining and railroad work who harbored conflicted impulses but also leaned, as workers, to the left. The social climate of Southeast Kansas, for instance, saw a geographical and political divide between local Republicans interested in agriculture and local miners, a normative divide, which fueled the second-generation miners' Americanizing impulses. *The Independent*, for its part, leaned left when necessary, even coming out in favor of the Russian Revolution.

Located twenty-five miles away from Mulberry and *The Independent*, in the small farming community of Girard, Crawford County's county seat—which boasted an up-and-coming Klan of its own—Marcet and Emanuel Haldeman-Julius owned and operated one of the world's largest radical publishing companies. Despite international success that would approach the half-billion sales point with the couple's new line of Little Blue Books, the Haldeman-Juliuses struggled to find a local readership, especially as *The Independent* worked to displace them as the central local organ of labor news.

The Haldeman-Juliuses, too, as a matter of course, supported the Russian Revolution and were naturally perplexed and disconcerted by the developing affiliation between local labor and the Klan. In fact, in 1931, after the Klan had been "ousted" from Kansas, Marcet Haldeman-Julius attempted to double down on socialism and reinvest the public in the socialist cause. With the help of her aunt, social reformer and Nobel Laureate Jane Addams—who sent advance letters to important government functionaries—traveled to the Soviet Union to offer extended coverage of the state of post-revolution Russia for all the comrades back home, her investment of the workingman's plight having been forged early in the kiln of her aunt's Hull House work and transferred to her publishing and writing endeavors, despite her husband's push, after 1929, away from socialism and toward a more economically viable populism that her husband valued. "Hull House" after all, "was founded only two years after Haldeman-Julius's birth, and the two grew up together, both, as it seemed, in Addams's shadow" (Barrett-Fox, 16), and her service there left an indelible mark. Living and working on Halstead Street each summer as a young woman imparted to Haldeman-Julius a sense of the transformative social presence women were beginning to establish in the early years of the twentieth century.

Having in 1921 acquired *The Appeal to Reason*, the seventh largest socialist weekly in the United States, the Haldeman-Juliuses were both a power-couple in the national leftist media scene and rather outcasts in an otherwise conservative state. Emanuel Julius came to *Appeal* early on as an editor, after serving on the staff of John Reed's *New York Call*, Carl Sandburg's *Los Angeles Citizen*, and Victor Berger's *Milwaukee Leader*, among others. Julius met his future wife, Marcet Haldeman, not long after his arrival, and realizing that she was a well-educated woman of means (she attended Bryn Mawr and the American Academy of Dramatic Arts), owner of the town bank, and a former New Yorker herself, pursued her. Marcet Haldeman at the time was working her way up the state of Kansas's Republican Party's political ladder. The niece and close friend to Jane Addams, she was infused from a young age with radical politics, largely because of her summers with Addams at Hull House. As, a decade earlier, Addams, W. E. B. DuBois, and James Weldon Johnson, along with other members of the newly formed NAACP, protested screenings of Griffith's *Birth of a Nation* and virtually shut down showings in many northern cities, Haldeman-Julius prepared in the middle twenties to fight the racism being pushed out of publications like *The*

Independent. She was not afraid to use her publishing empire and notoriety to do so, despite the low esteem in which it was held by locals.[15]

The consolidation of organized labor and the KKK was encouraged by *The Independent,* which had in 1925 the largest circulation of any weekly publication in Crawford County, far outdistancing *The Haldeman-Julius Weekly* in the race for a local readership. This large circulation was made possible by *The Independent's* ability to insinuate itself into the labor community by means of facilitating strong identifications with miners as Americans, asking for their dissociation from immigrant status and asking, in particular, for workers to identify with whiteness and the Klan's particularly monolithic version of the American dream. Since the first major wave of immigration occurred in Kansas in the 1880s, now the labor community consisted of the children of those miners who were willing to throw off their parents' Catholicism and to embrace the "100 percent American" rhetoric the KKK tendered, through the instantiation of groups targeted at winning over and protestantizing immigrants and their children.

> They declared that the "Invisible Empire" stood for Protestant, Fundamental Christianity, old-fashioned morality, and patriotism. At the same time, while arguing that the organization was not opposed to Catholics, Negroes, Jews, and the foreign-born, they nonetheless capitalized upon the prejudices held by many citizens towards these groups.[16]

The new Klan in Kansas operated a rhetorical machine that displaced hate rhetoric with language aimed at creating the tolerance for what they considered nothing more than natural inequalities: inequalities between blacks and whites as expressed in Jim Crow politics that also bled into Suffrage polices despite their efforts to undermine gender inequality between women and men. For instance, an August 29, 1924, article reminds readers, for instance, that

> Nature has ordained that the sexes have no equality . . . As the second in physical strength and mental regularity woman loses in her competition with man in his own field of life activity—usefulness or pleasure, but in her own sphere she is the queen of the earth and no man will deny it.[17]

Similarly, as H. A. Strong argues, embracing a similarly paternalistic racism,

> In the intermixing, and intercohabitating of the white and colored races the Negro without question has had the worst of it. . . . Purity of race should appeal to him in the same measure it should appeal to the white race, and DOES appeal to all right thinking, moral. . . . people of BOTH races. One of the BLACKEST chapters in American history has been the devilish, and demoralizing cohabitation between the two races. If there is a HELL the lowest pit in it should be reserved for the men and

women in America of BOTH the white and black races, who have contributed to the mixing of the races. A damnation deeper than HELL itself is due them . . . [T]here is NO good reason why the Negro should be Anti-Klan at all. He is being duped by bunco steerers like White into an anti-Klan attitude.[18]

This "tolerant" rhetoric of natural inequality that were affirmed in eugenic teachings combined with statements debasing those members of the national Klan that committed hate crimes coalesced with other hot button issues in Crawford County, like religion, to win over a significant percentage of the population. In August of 1924, Orin Strong argued in *The Independent*, "In fact the 4000 Klansmen in Crawford County are the same men and young men they were before the joined the Klan. Just as with any church membership there are many who stumble and fall," but those "who have joined the Klan for a lark, or to get even with some enemy have been sorely disappointed."[19]

By the mid-twenties, the Haldeman-Juliuses found themselves the targets of *The Independent* and its Klan interests due to their competition with the former for the labor market readers, their anti-racist views, their atheistic and pro-women stance, and for what editors of *The Independent* considered a general distaste for American ideals. At the heart of their distaste for American ideals lived a belief in the relationship between racial equality and labor. Noting the important connection between race and labor in Kansas, Haldeman-Julius wanted to state her position very clearly and publicly: she was "entirely opposed to the segregation of races" and believed that African Americans "should have the same privileges in schools, in traveling, in restaurants, in theaters, in stores, in libraries, [and] . . . *most especially in labor unions!*"[20]

Focusing his attack, Orin Strong implies in *The Independent* that something sinister must be going on with a couple who publishes a Blue Book titled "On the Myth of Nordic Supremacy" and who "virtually proves" the "white race" is "inferior to races of color" (1), calling the Haldeman-Julius stance on race a great inferiority complex. Additionally, in another editorial referencing the couple's hundred-million-selling Little Blue Books, Orin Strong calls the Haldeman-Juliuses "superficial scandalmongers [who] would knock the prop down that holds the building up."[21] Strong continues, referring again to one of the Haldeman-Julius Blue Books and offering his own historical précis,

> The White man—the long blond, did not subdue the jungle and the Polar regions by accident. He did it by design. He has left his impress by force and blarney—employing either with equal vim and purpose. If he succumbs to the Yellows, the Browns and the Blacks, it will be because he is too well fed, and not because nature did not endow him with superlative mind and body. He may be deteriorating, but if so he hasn't shown it. We had our Yellow Perils, and many other alarms, but the high seas and the solid ground [are] still the playgrounds of the

blond Nordic. A mighty man was the Roman Centurian—mind and
arms were strong, but the Savage Nordic conquered him in the end—
because he was stronger . . . [Those] who ridicule the Nordics, merely
prove the "Sour Grapes" fable; they recite what they want and not
what is. The Nordic may be a hypocrite, but he is not an imbecile. Mr.
Julius lambasts suppression. Even so he thrives because there is no real
suppression in this Land of the Free and Home of the Brave.[22]

Here, of course, the Americanizing impulse associate with pioneering
utopias dissolves into a kind of metanarrative of racial supremacy with a
subtext pining for contemporary opportunities for suppression.

While *The Independent*'s writers berated Emanuel Haldeman-Julius for
his un-American belief in the equality of different races, they all but
missed his wife's emergent but radical message, ostensibly due to her
gender identity (as well, perhaps, as Emanuel's proclivity to seek the
spotlight and serve as the face of the Haldeman-Julius's publishing empire). The editors of *The Independent* and the leaders of the Klan shared an
attitude that women were unthreatening, unthinking, and unable to deal
with questions of political or philosophical heft. Her perceived invisibil-
ity, to a degree, motived Haldeman-Julius, serving as an impetus to develop a systematic response to *The Independent*'s message.

A WOMAN OF ACTION: MARCET HALDEMAN-JULIUS'S
REFORM WORK

Haldeman-Julius's impetus for action was personal as well as melioristic:
when Orin Strong focuses his attacks on Emanuel, if his wife is mentioned, not only is her name purposively misspelled, her role in the
Haldeman-Julius publishing company is downplayed or overlooked.
Only her wealth is of significance to Strong, as it evidences Emanuel's
propensity to scam. His gullible wife's status is downgraded to just another victim of his manipulative agenda. One of Strong's principle *ad
hominems* centered on Emanuel's desire to court Haldeman-Julius's for-
tune in order to help himself to "one of the famous estates of this section"
and to propel himself to national fame and attention.[23] While Strong's
characterizations of Julius's motives may not fall far from the truth—he
could not have purchased *The Appeal to Reason* without his wife's sub-
stantial contribution—they obscure her capacity for meaningful social
engagement under her husband's hubris.

As *The Independent* characterizes things, Haldeman-Julius falls victim
to "the whole Julius process of marrying an heiress and gradually acquir-
ing control of the property," which serves as "the great inspiration behind Mr. Julius's ethereal flights of mentality."[24] She succumbs to her
wayward husband, abandoning the "harmonious . . . Girard girl . . . who

once entertained ideas of American idealism," an indirect reference to Haldeman-Julius's well-known relationship with Jane Addams. Haldeman-Julius's status devolves to, simply, the victim of a literary grift.[25]

Haldeman-Julius's epistolary indicates otherwise, demonstrating a sense of her own political and economic exigencies. Writing to Addams upon the occasion of her 1916 marriage: "[H]ere I am, a good Republican, planning and working for the success of the largest and most powerful Socialist paper in the U.S., the largest and one of the most powerful in the world I guess," but, she explains, "[w]hen the editorial board meets . . . I seem to quit being myself and see things altogether as Manuel's wife. For the time being," she elaborates, "I accept this point of view," but "[j]ust what effect it is going to have on my character, I can't say."[26] As her discomfort with Emanuel's reign grows throughout his several infidelities of the 1920s and her status as his wife erodes, Haldeman-Julius increasingly rebels. Strong, however, despite evidence to the contrary, relegates Haldeman-Julius, even eight years into her marriage, to object-status, explaining "[t]he Haldeman tragedy is exciting much community pathos—even compassion on the part of those who believe the accomplished wife to be a victim of the vaulting ambition of an unscrupulous adventurer."[27]

As Allen's attempted ouster ignited the Klan, *The Independent*'s softening of Marcet Haldeman-Julius motivated her to pursue her own agenda regarding racism in Kansas. Rather than risk taking on *The Independent* and appearing to engage in a war for readers, a move that might appear to devalue the central question of racism in her home state, Haldeman-Julius began a campaign to support Kansas's African American students.

Focusing on the state of Kansas meant Haldeman-Julius taking herself out of her sphere of influence and focusing closely on her place of origin, a location often ignored by Emanuel. Her work evinced a grassroots capacity for empathy and action completely overlooked by her husband, one much more akin to the work done by her aunt. As Addams wrote in *Twenty Years at Hull House*, published five years before the Haldeman-Julius's marriage, justice must begin at home, must be rooted in places of being. And "[i]t must," despite its local origins, she explains, "be grounded in a philosophy whose foundation is on the solidarity of the human race."[28] She continues by reminding us that racism and its desiccating tentacles spread to every corner of human existence. "We all bear traces," Addams argues, "of the starvation struggle which for so long made up the life of race."[29]

> Our very organism holds memories and glimpses of that long life of our ancestors which still goes on among so many of our contemporaries. Nothing so deadens the sympathies and shrivels the power of enjoyment, as the persistent keeping away from the great opportunities for helpfulness and a continual ignoring of the starvation struggle, which makes up the life of at least half the race.[30]

Perhaps partially through her combative entanglement with the editors of *The Independent*, Haldeman-Julius acted upon Addams's insight: that racism is economic as well as ideological and represents a negative educational paradigm, a great sleight of hand concomitant with the preservation and guarantee of slight means. And in the 1920s, the Klan's cultural program was thriving and demanded recourse.

TO LAWRENCE WITH LOVE: TAKING ON THE UNIVERSITY OF KANSAS

By 1927, the year of Haldeman-Julius's response to the KKK's "conflagration" in eastern Kansas, racial animosity had built throughout the state, ranging from Southeast Kansas all the way up to the Northeast tip of the state, Lawrence, the seat of Douglas County. In fact, in 1924, for instance, "the Kansas Klan held a statewide conference at the Bowersock Theater, and Massachusetts Street was lined with the klansmens' cars."[31] Unfortunately, this type of gathering was a relatively common sight on Lawrence's main thoroughfare, Massachusetts Street, despite Lawrence's abolitionist origins. The sentiment climbed Mt. Oread and into the halls of the University of Kansas.

Racism at the university was a huge problem in the 1920s, but its status as a problem was undercut by the pedantic institutional recourse of Jim Crow: mutual separation, less a solution than an alibi. To name merely a few institutional slights, African American students were "barred from intercollegiate athletics, the glee club, the band, and the orchestra, not to mention the debating team, ROTC, and the student council;" additionally, black students were barred from university housing, and "no white fraternity or sorority would pledge an African American."[32] When black students wanted to attend public university events, they were kept separate from the white students and often given seats with restricted views. While this was an acceptable social fact for most whites in the community (and in the administration), this was an actionable item for Marcet Haldeman-Julius, one that offered legitimacy, publicity, and transparency. More important, it was one that had the potential to transform educational futures.

By this time in the late 1920s Haldeman-Julius had sold tens of thousands of Little Blue Books and had published two successful novels that had been translated into several languages: she had an audience ready to be activated, an audience listening to her, not her husband.[33] She had the traction—and the audience—to make a public stand against the increasing power of the Klan and the more diffuse power of racism in Kansas.

Shocked by an essay by University of Kansas student Loren Miller entitled "Unrest among the Negro Students in a White College: The University of Kansas" that appeared in the August 1927 edition of the *Crisis*, the national publication of the NAACP under the editorship of W. E. B. Du Bois, Haldeman-Julius turned her immediate attention to battling institutional racism at the University of Kansas, where her son, Henry, would eventually matriculate. Miller, who would go on to be a respected NAACP litigator, judge, and civil rights activist in California, relayed his abuse at the hands of the institution, arguing that even though "Kansas stands high in education" and "is a pioneer in social reform and uplift," numerous racial injustices occur every day at the University under the guidance of "paternalistic racist" Chancellor E. H. Lindley, even though "it is one of his boasts that he comes from abolitionist stock."[34]

Rather than continue to argue race with the staff of *The Independent*, whose racism and sexism remained intractable, Haldeman-Julius set about writing an indictment of the administration of the University of Kansas, targeting an institution with potential for change, one committed to setting community standards. She sent letters asking for explanations and meetings to Lindley and Dr. Forrest C. "Phog" Allen. Lindley, a noted psychologist and former president of the American Association of University Presidents, complied—as did Coach Allen. In a prompt response dated September 30, 1927, the Chancellor stated that "As a pupil of David Starr Jordan, Stanley Hall, and William James, I have thought of myself as a humanist. But no doubt age and 'capitalistic control' have wrought a change."[35] Though he does not specify what changes have been wrought by "capitalistic control," the context of the letter inspired Haldeman-Julius to inquire more deeply about what economic structures Lindley took for granted. She was shocked at the response. Lindley explains,

> In our cafeteria they [African Americans] are welcome, and are enjoying service which they recognize they cannot have with a wide-open policy. They have agreed to limit themselves to a rather large section of the cafeteria, where friendly whites also may come . . . This restriction . . . is made necessary by the failure to maintain otherwise a sufficient volume of business to keep the cafeteria going . . . One of the problems yet unsolved here is that of simultaneous use of the swimming pool by blacks and whites. [For that problem, w]e have not found a satisfactory solution. (Lindley)

The problem of the swimming pool was shaped a bit different, however, in Loren Miller's *Crisis* article. Miller claimed that "[c]olored students, men and women, are absolutely refused permission to use the state-owned swimming pool."[36] And it was not only the swimming pool that was off limits, for as Miller writes, that though it:

> is natural that colored students should seek places on athletic teams. They are absolutely refused any place whatever. Dr. F. C. Allen, head of athletics, said recently that no colored man will ever have a chance

as long as he is there. Complaints to the Chancellor meet no considera-
tion, as he avows his support of the present athletic regime. [37]

Allen's intolerance around issues of race was absolute, though his legacy
as a beloved figure at the university (cf. his statue outside Allen Field-
house, perhaps the most famous college basketball venue in the country)
has obscured the exact nature of his tenure at the university. Well into the
1940s, for instance, Allen participated in blatantly racist comic theatricals
performed for white students and posed for pictures in which his team
donned blackface. [38] When interviewed by Haldeman-Julius, Allen sof-
tened his views a bit, denying Miller's charges but adding that he did
"not believe that colored and white boys should play together in any
games of physical contact or combat." [39] Lindley ended his letter with
respect for Haldeman-Julius, writing,

> While I have long been a friend of your Blue Books, usually carrying
> some with me when I travel, I have never had the pleasure of meeting
> you. When you come to Lawrence I should be glad if you would call at
> my office and give me the pleasure of acquaintance with you. [40]

Faced with this disturbing information and some contradictory claims,
Haldeman-Julius set out to do more research and to draw more public
attention to the cause, enlisting the help of Jane Addams's old friends
James Weldon Johnson and W. E. B. Du Bois of the NAACP. Having
collected more data on not only racism at the University of Kansas but at
all the state funded colleges in Kansas, Haldeman-Julius began preparing
for a trip to visit Lindley and to advocate for equality of treatment. She
wrote James Weldon Johnson, that as "Kansas is my native state and the
Chancellor says that he thinks of himself as a humanist, I am hoping my
visit and article may bring about some practical results." [41]

The product of her visit was an article for the January 1928 edition of
the *Haldeman-Julius Monthly* in which she took the Lindley administration
to task for its willful ignorance of subtle and not so subtle forms of racism
at the University. She explained,

> With [Miller's] article literally in my hands, I checked each accusation
> he had made and [with the exception of two items that had been
> changed since] every charge of his was borne out accurately by the
> facts . . . [T]he narrowest, most oppressive, most provincially astigmatic
> atmosphere of all is to be found at the University which should lead the
> others in culture and breadth of vision. The irony of this is that its
> Chancellor, Dr. Ernest H. Lindley, who possesses distinction both in
> mind and appearance, is not only the most scholarly and cultivated of
> all the Kansas presidents, but as a pupil of David Starr Jordan, Stanley
> Hall, and William James, wishes to be, feels himself to be, and essen-
> tially is—a humanist. [42]

Not missing the irony in Lindley's self-assessment, Haldeman-Julius continued to address his cafeteria policy. In defense of the new, segregated cafeteria

> Dr. Lindley explained to me that the old cafeteria in which there was no segregation had run a deficit. (But for the last two years at least, the food was poor; the prices high.) . . . "If this cafeteria has to close there would be no place in which the colored students could eat," Dr. Lindley further pointed out. "What would be better?" He takes the position—quite sincerely, I am sure—that he is obliged to choose between segregating the Negroes or eliminating them entirely from the cafeteria if it is to continue. He insists that the lack of segregation has always been a constant financial disadvantage . . . The whole atmosphere of Lawrence is so prejudice-saturated that it may be true . . . If it really will not pay without segregation then it should be closed until the atmosphere has become such that it can be opened under conditions that are equal to all the students . . . A few weeks inconvenience would, I suspect, be quite enough.[43]

At the base of Lindley's argument for segregating the cafeteria, an important issue arises: he volunteers subservience to those elements of "capitalistic control" to which he alluded in his earlier letter to Haldeman-Julius, using economics as a buffer for criticism and simultaneously a cipher for making the University of Kansas's institutional racism seem innocuous. This reasoning was, for Haldeman-Julius, logically circular and morally pernicious.

Taking Lindley's assumption to task, Haldeman-Julius asserted that "it is the consensus of opinion that it is only because of the [prejudice of the] Lawrence people that the Negro students at the University must be humiliated."[44] As a publisher, author, radical socialist, post-liberal feminist, and mother of a Kansas University student Haldeman-Julius burned at the debilitating treatment of African Americans there. Kansas University, she explained,

> truckles shamelessly to the prejudices of the people of Lawrence . . . Many counties, you should realize, have one or two such towns. There is no blinking the fact of this . . . prejudice . . . in our midst. Its activity is due in large part to the conflagration the Ku Klux Klan recently attempted to set ablaze.[45]

In 1920s Kansas, economic agency and racial superiority impinged upon each other. As demonstrated previously, even organized labor on the far left—consisting of the grown children of immigrants—was becoming more conservative and heeding the call for racial distinctiveness. The Klan represented for them some economic solvency, and thus, as in Lindley's position, economics in Kansas both buffered racist strategies by creating lexicons of acceptability for them and lubricated pathways to further crimes against African Americans. The University of Kansas, the great bastion of learning on the plains, led by one of the country's most preeminent scholars, was not immune to this subtle plague of racism articulated through the rhetoric of economic individualism and community responsibility. This subtle admission of racism on Lindley's part is ironic and disconcerting because Lindley's mentor was the famous pragmatist psychologist William James, a staunch supporter of pluralism.

In this case, Haldeman-Julius and her radical publishing machinery exposed for a white readership that may not have been reading *The Crisis* the university administration's economic justifications for its continued social violence. Haldeman-Julius's work against racism coincided with the fall of the KKK in Kansas in the late 1920s, but it did not fully facilitate that fall. Internal strife over money and violence did that, but Haldeman-Julius's inquiries and articles about the University of Kansas went a great distance in attracting attention to the situation in Kansas. In fact, riding the wave of criticism that began with Loren Miller's article and then was taken up by Haldeman-Julius, "[i]n 1930, Dr. W. E. B. Du Bois, the noted scholar, author, and editor . . . wrote Chancellor Lindley to inquire about these criticisms of KU's racial policies."[46] Lindley, shockingly, continued to support Allen and the racist politics at the University Kansas, and these practices did not even end with the Lindley administration. Though he retired in 1939, his successor, Deane W. Mallott, soon "demonstrated that he was committed to the perpetuation of the University's politics of black exclusion" as well.[47]

Haldeman-Julius's work on behalf of African American students in Kansas was not in vain, though, as indicated by sustained and impassioned reader responses from fellow Kansans; her fight for policy changes also served as a clarion call for educational transparency along the lines of racial justice and served, therefore, as a humanizing force for African Americans all over the state. As one Kansas University student, F. Cornel Webster, wrote to Haldeman-Julius in November of 1927, "we are still thinking of you here and feel much better off for having met you."[48] As another correspondent, Amos Baker, expressed in November, 1927,

> I note with great interest, some of the statements you made and congratulate you for having the backbone to express your news concerning the Negros that attend these institutions and also that interest you are taking in my people.[49]

Baker continues,

> I am interested in this matter because I have two girls one of whom will finish Topeka high this June and wife and I are thinking of sending her to one of these schools you mentioned but if what you say is true, and I do not doubt your word, I am asking you for some advice [as to whether to send her] . . . I know you are interested in the Negroes [sic] welfare or you would not have taken the time or the energy to make

this investigation. Thanking you in advance for the interest you have shown in our poor struggling race and pray to God that you may give some way to help us be looked up[on] as men and women.[50]

As a highly literate white woman of means with a public voice, Haldeman-Julius was certainly in a better position that most African Americans in the state to force an audience with university administrators and sway public opinion. Her decision to speak out was borne of the gendered silencing gestures she encountered simultaneously in disputes over race and labor with *The Independent* in 1924, and her response—her move to "go local"—was pragmatically influenced by Jane Addams, even though it stood in radical juxtaposition to her husband's national and international publishing priorities. And while Haldeman-Julius never saw her life in danger, as the nineteen African Americans lynched in Kansas between 1882 and 1968 did, she nonetheless made herself a target for the Klan in Eastern Kansas.

Though it facilitated Haldeman-Julius's detection of the connection between economics and racism in Kansas, her socialism, in this instance, took a back seat to liberal values like her aunt's. Indeed, Jane Addams's influence is, if anything, the defining narrative by which history should understand Haldeman-Julius's radical transformation from socialite to social justice advocate. And in this role Haldeman-Julius reflects Addams's impulse toward social engagement: both women served others, to some degree, out of a desire to create or recreate a sense of place, a sense of home, which is why that, even while international issues concerned both reformers, their primary action took place within the bounds of the local, the immediate communities in which they acted and through which they emerged as leaders for social justice. Both women gain authority through service and through work and engaged meaningfully in the period's most pressing social concerns. Indeed both Jane and Haldeman-Julius "viewed work as a means of exertion and self-expression, as a way of adding the spark of [their] own divinity to [a] universe" otherwise devoid of the deific.[51] An entry into Addams's college journal characterized the two women's positions very well: a person will "never feel at home in the world save through labor; [s]he who does not labor is homeless."[52]

REVISITING THE MIDDLE BORDER

Whether the interest was killing labor or promoting racial equality, both Henry Allen and Marcet Haldeman-Julius understood that Kansas held a special place on the middle border and that the border was shifting, not geographically but politically and temporally. In many ways the bellwether of national politics, Kansas functioned in the 1920s as a cultural

laboratory, particularly the eastern part of the state, where a rich abolitionist history—one that came with the founding of Lawrence, KS by
abolitionists from Lawrence, MA—crumbled, facing changing generational tides, with most of the original settlers from "Bleeding Kansas"
having passed away.[53] The story of racial politics in Kansas in the 1920s is
textured not only by Allen's and Haldeman-Julius's work but that of
journalist and reformer William Allen White and many others, but the
stories together represent an important and complex strain of American
anti-racism, one that in its incomplete becoming, in its emergence
through events like *Brown v. the Board of Education* in 1954, placed Kansas,
again and again, at the epicenter of important social change.

NOTES

1. William Tuttle, "Separate but Not Equal: African Americans and the 100-year
Struggle for Equality in Lawrence and at the University of Kansas, 1850s–1960," *Embattled Lawrence*, Eds. Dennis Domer and Barbara Watkins (Lawrence: University of
Kansas Press, 1988), 139.
2. I wish to thank Bayliss Harsh, Brian Moss, and Caitlyn Donnelly of the University of Kansas's Library System, as well as Randy Roberts, Dean of Library Services/
Special Collections at Pittsburg State University. My thanks, too, go out to Lin Frede-
rickson at the Kansas State Historical Society.
3. Lila Lee Jones, "The Ku Klux Klan in eastern Kansas during the 1920s" (MA
thes. Emporia Kansas State College, 1975). 7
4. Jones, 9.
5. Charles Wilson Sloan, "Kansas Battles the Invisible Empire: The Legal Ouster of
the KKK from Kansas, 1922–1927," *Kansas Historical Quarterly* 40 no. 3 (1974): 394.
6. Dominico Gagliardo, "The Gompers-Allen Debate on the Kansas Industrial
Court," *Kansas History* 3 no. 4 (1934): 386.
7. Charles Wilson Sloan, "Kansas Battles," 393.
8. *The New Republic*, 5
9. Sloan, 395.
10. Jones, 5.
11. Jones, 12.
12. Dominico Gagliardo, ""The Gompers-Allen Debate on the Kansas Industrial
Court." *Kansas History*. 3.4 (1934): 387.
13. Sloan, 401.
14. Evidence suggests that before its demise, the Klan had a stronger presence in
Kansas than previously thought. Even the *Independent*, whose editorial staff supported
the Klan's "100 percent American" program that advocated against "the intermarriage
and intercohabitation and intermixing of the races," toward the end of "purity of race"
and denigrated Catholics and Jews, believed that the pro-Klan Republican candidate,
Ben Paulen, would lose the 1924 gubernatorial race to Jonathon Davis, a Democrat
who, though he had had Klan support in the past, aligned himself with the national
party and denounced the Klan. The reason the editors at the *Independent* believed this
was because William Allen White, certainly one of the most famous Kansans—and a
proud Republican—was running against Paulen as an Independent, hoping to split
the Republican ticket and show his Republican party that the KKK was not a political

asset. Writing for the *Independent*, H. A. Strong speculated that Davis, the incumbent, chose a smarter path by downplaying the issue of the KKK while William Allen White and Ben Paulen fought over it. Though ideologically, the *Independent* supported Paulen, they thought his explicitly pro-Klan status would damage his campaign. Needless to say, they were surprised when Paulen won, despite William Allen White pulling over 150,000 of 600,000 votes cast away from the Republican ticket. That Paulen could win speaks volumes toward the political weight and popular sympathy the Invisible Empire had in 1924 Kansas.

15. Emanuel Haldeman-Julius, who directed most of the company's publishing endeavors with his wife serving as an author, advisor, and partial owner, held little interest in the locale of his publishing company (chosen initially by Julius Wayland, owner of *The Appeal to Reason*, not for its radical politics or affinity with labor issues but for its access to the railroad and the potential to distribute papers on the cheap), and to an extent, he cultivated the local workers' reciprocal disinterest. Aside from Marcet's significant work with children of miners in Girard, work patterned upon Addams's work with immigrant children at Hull House, the company focused exclusively on issues beyond its own county.

16. Sloan, 393.

17. Orin Strong, "The Women Folks," *The Independent*, August 29, 1924.

18. H. A. Strong, "Bunkum Bill White and Other Bunk," *The Independent*, September 24, 1924: 7.

19. Orin Strong "The Women Folks," 5.

20. Marcet Haldeman-Julius, *Talks with Joseph McCabe and Other Confidential Sketches* (Girard, KS: Haldeman-Julius Publishing Company, 1931), 72.

21. Orin Strong "The Women Folks," 1.

22. Orin Strong, "The Blue Books," *The Independent*, Feb. 12, 1926, 1.

23. Strong, "The Blue Books," 1.

24. Strong, "The Blue Books," 2.

25. Strong, "The Blue Books," 2.

26. Jason Barrett-Fox, "A Rhetorical Recovery: Self-Avowal and Self-Displacement in the Life, Fiction, and Nonfiction of Marcet Haldeman-Julius, 1921–1936," *Rhetoric Review* 21 no.1 (2010):16.

27. Orin Strong, "The Women Folk," 2.

28. Jane Addams, *Twenty Years at Hull House* (New York: MacMillan, 1911), 126.

29. Addams, 116.

30. Addams, 116.

31. Tuttle, "Separate but not Equal," 145.

32. Tuttle, "Separate but not Equal," 145.

33. Emanuel Haldeman-Julius, *The First Hundred Million*, (New York: Simon and Schuster, 1928), 12–16.

34. Tuttle, "Separate but not Equal," 145; and Loren Miller, "The Unrest among Negro Students at a White College: The University of Kansas," *The Crisis* 34 (1927): 187.

35. E. H. Lindley, letter to Marcet Haldeman-Julius, September 30, 1927.

36. Loren Miller, "The Unrest among Negro Students at a White College: The University of Kansas." *The Crisis* 34 (1927): 187.

37. Miller, "Unrest among Negro Students," 187.

38. Tuttle, "Separate but not Equal," 146.

39. Tuttle, "Separate but not Equal," 146.

40. Lindley, letter, 1927.

41. Marcet Haldeman-Julius, letter to James Weldon Johnson, October 12, 1927.

42. Marcet Haldeman-Julius, "What the Negro Students in Kansas Endure." *The Haldeman-Julius Monthly* 7 no. 2 (1928): 7–8.

43. Haldeman-Julius, "Students," 11.

44. Haldeman-Julius, "Students," 15.

45. Haldeman-Julius, "Students," 14.

46. Tuttle, "Separate but not Equal," 148.

47. Tuttle, "Separate but not Equal," 146.

48. Dustin Gann, "Written in Black and White: Creating an Ideal America, 1919–1970," (PhD Diss., U of Kansas. 2012), 61.

49. Gann, "Written in Black and White," 61–62.

50. Gann, "Written in Black and White," 62.

51. Victoria Bissell Brown, *The Education of Jane Addams* (Philadelphia: University of Pennsylvania Press, 2003), 82.

52. Addams 82.

53. Tuttle, "Separate but not Equal," 145.

SIX

No Place like Home

Chicago's Black Metropolis and the Johnson Publishing Offices, 1942–1975

James West

First published in 1945, St. Clair Drake and Horace R. Cayton's *Black Metropolis* quickly became a seminal study of race and urban life in the United States.[1] The authors outlined how an influx of Southern black migrants into the "Midwest Metropolis" during the first half of the twentieth century had birthed a second metropolis—a "Black Metropolis." Known alternatively as Bronzeville, this enclave was located on the city's South Side; a "unique and distinctive city within a city" where the vast majority of Chicago's black population lived and worked.[2] The city's deeply entrenched patterns of segregation—enforced by restrictive housing covenants and systemic racial prejudice—had levied a heavy social, political and economic burden on its black residents. Yet it also created a vibrant and self-sustaining community which allowed black businesses, media outlets and "race enterprises" to flourish.[3]

One of the most iconic and enduring enterprises to emerge out of Chicago's African American community was the Johnson Publishing Company, founded in 1942 by John H. Johnson.[4] In the years and decades since the introduction of his first publication *Negro Digest*, Johnson developed an array of magazines such as *Ebony*, *Jet*, and *Tan Confessions* which sought to give voice to the diversity and complexity of the black community on a local and national scale.[5] This was rooted in the Company's public image as a black owned and oriented business, which had developed within the unique atmosphere of Bronzeville. As the

Company expanded so too did its base of operations—from a corner office in the Supreme Life Insurance building to a custom built headquarters on the Chicago Loop which offered "a visual pronouncement that black America had arrived in all its striving, outrageous, hip and fashionable glory."[6]

However, even as this transition was celebrated as a symbol for the gains made by blacks in the years since World War II, it served to distance the Company from the heart of the Black Metropolis, the Bronzville neighborhood of Chicago, which had fostered its rise.

This chapter explores how these intersections of race and space informed popular representations of the Johnson Publishing headquarters between the Company's formation in 1942 and its move to 820 South Michigan Avenue in the early 1970s. I argue that the image of Johnson's magazines as influential voices for the black community was intimately connected to the Company's physical location and building history, and rooted in the image of Bronzeville as a symbolic space that articulated the philosophies of the New Negro Movement for black business innovation and cultural production. By functioning as an important physical symbol for black achievement, the Company's offices became an important part of Johnson's editorial emphasis on middle-class aspiration and racial uplift. At the same time, they reified the limitations of this editorial philosophy and the continuing impact of racial segregation and inequality within Chicago's Black Metropolis during the years since World War II.

LITERATURE REVIEW

As William Gleason has noted, while race continues to be one of the most central analytical and theoretical categories for literary studies and American history more broadly, it has often been overlooked in the interdisciplinary study of architecture and literature.[7] This is reflective of biases within architectural history and theory, where the "the makers and users of architecture have been overwhelmingly positioned as white both historically and culturally."[8] However, over the past few decades a number of different scholars have looked to examine the connections between race as a social construct and its impact upon the architectural profession in new ways—be this through a recognition of the parallels between architecture and blackness as aesthetic and linguistic practices, or through a historical recovery of pioneering black architects.[9] Unpacking the connections between design, racial identity, and community empowerment help to highlight how black architects and engineers have performed a "balancing act of accommodation, resistance, and appropriation" through their designs and buildings.[10]

We can link such research to the broader intersections of race, geography, urban politics and cultural production in American history. Scholars such as Diane Harris and June Manning Thomas have highlighted the powerful ways in which race has informed our understanding and production of the built environment.[11] From a different perspective, the creative expression which emerged out of the Harlem Renaissance and the Chicago Black Renaissance provide us with powerful examples of the complex and constantly changing relationship between "artistry and space."[12] This has most frequently been explored on an individual level—through the Harlem of James Baldwin and Louis Armstrong, or the Bronzeville of Archibald Motley and Gwendolyn Brooks.[13] Yet it can also be applied to the relationship between ethnocentric institutions, the spaces they inhabit and the communities they serve.

Accordingly, an investigation of the relationship between the physical site of Johnson Publishing and the editorial philosophy of its publications can offer us new ways of thinking about the company's "unique place in African-American cultural history."[14] In looking to explore this relationship I take my cue from the recent work of Aurora Wallace. In her 2012 study *Media Capital*, the author illustrated how a range of New York based publishers have historically utilized both the architecture of their offices and their physical location to "convey permanence, authority, and stability to their readers, and to lend much needed creditability to their enterprises."[15] However, Wallace can be argued to have neglected the role of race and ethnicity in her analysis of such "media architecture." For example, she rationalizes the move uptown by publications such as the *New York Times* around the turn of the twentieth century as an attempt to distinguish themselves from the "cheap and vulgar scandal papers" of Park Row—yet this move could also be seen as a retreat from the expanding ethnic and racial enclaves of Chinatown, Little Italy, and the Lower East Side.[16]

Drawing from and expanding on Wallace's work, I argue that Johnson Publishing utilized the spaces it inhabited to substantiate its image as a conscientious representative of and voice for black communities on a local, national and international scale. In the same way that New York newspapers used their buildings to emphasize their civic responsibility, Johnson Publishing presented its buildings as key sites for black communal representation and development. In contrast to Gleason's notion of "sites unseen" therefore, the buildings of Johnson Publishing operated as explicitly visible spaces which looked to legitimate and valorize black cultural production, and which extended and reinforced the Company's editorial emphasis on black achievement and racial uplift.[17]

BUILDING THE BLACK METROPOLIS

As a distinct black community began to coalesce within Chicago during the first decades of the twentieth century, black leaders such as Oscar DePriest promoted the development of independent black institutions which would help to "uplift the race."[18] Faced with overt racism and extreme segregation, black Chicagoans forged their own "unique sense of modernity" through cultural production and the development of a self-contained business community.[19] Robert Silverman has argued that racial discrimination in Chicago actually provided a competitive advantage for black businesses by necessitating the development of a self-contained marketplace. The continuing influx of black migrants ensured that the city's black businesses thrived despite being "essentially cut off from the economic and social mainstream of the rest of the city."[20]

One of the most influential "race enterprises" to emerge out of this period was the *Chicago Defender*, a black weekly newspaper founded in 1905 by Robert Sengstacke Abbott. By the outbreak of World War One the *Defender* had become the nation's most influential black newspaper, with a vast national readership. Through editorials and political cartoons, Abbott condemned racial oppression and enthusiastically endorsed Chicago as a destination for black migrants.[21] This was supplemented by endeavors such as his "Great Northern Drive" of 1917, which publicized specially discounted trains which would bring black sojourners north.[22] The efforts of Abbot and the *Defender* fed into an explosion in the city's black population. Between 1910 and the outbreak of World War II Chicago's black population increased from around 40,000 to over a quarter of a million, creating the Black Metropolis depicted by Drake and Cayton.[23]

If the *Defender* had served as the pre-eminent voice for black Americans on a local and national scale during the first half of the twentieth century, then this role was arguably taken up by Johnson's publications in the post-war years, and in particular *Ebony* magazine. Following its introduction in November 1945 *Ebony* quickly became the largest selling black publication in the country, with a circulation, readership and influence that dwarfed traditional black newspapers.[24] Johnson's editorial vision offered a departure from the traditional modus operandi of the black press as an uncompromising voice of protest.[25] He promised to celebrate the "happier side of negro life" and to promote images of "lifestyle and its material accomplishments" as a route to racial uplift and respectability.[26] This philosophy was criticized by black intellectuals such as E. Franklin Frazier, but met a receptive audience. In celebrating black achievement through the acquisition of prestige and monetary wealth, Johnson's magazines tapped into the expectation for change created by World War II.[27]

Whereas the editorial philosophy of Johnson's publications may have differed from that of the *Defender*, Johnson followed the newspaper's lead

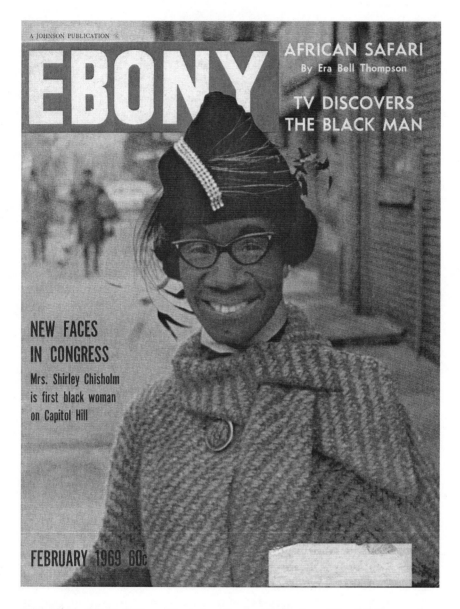

Figure 6.1.   Cover of *Ebony* Magazine. Source: Collection of the U.S House of
Representatives.

in utilizing the city's appeal as a major black enclave. Sengstacke had
exploited the *Defender*'s location in Chicago to promote the city as an
important racial enclave, and by extension the significance of his newspaper as the voice of the city's black population. Similarly, Johnson connected his publications' role as important outlets for black expression and

representation to the city's perceived racial exceptionalism. He would later declare that Chicago was for southern blacks "what Mecca was to the Moslems and what Jerusalem was to the Jews: a place of magic and mirrors and dreams."[28] James Grossman has argued that despite the lure of Harlem it was Chicago "that captured the attention and imagination of restless black Americans" in much of the Deep South.[29] Whilst Johnson's magazines would take up and surpass the *Defender*'s coverage on a national and international scale, their value was similarly "rooted in black Chicago institutions and topics."[30]

Furthermore, although his magazines maintained an upbeat editorial perspective, Johnson recognized the challenges faced by Chicago's black citizens, including himself.[31] Like Drake and Cayton, he understood the Black Metropolis to be simultaneously an impoverished and crime-ridden ghetto, and a vibrant racial enclave, which boasted "its own cultural and economic institutions, its own business, professional, and political leadership, and its own intellectual and artistic elite."[32] This duality— "the tragedy of racism and the triumph of black persistence in the face of racial exclusion"—provided a dual rationale for the success of his publications.[33] The emphasis on black achievement and the gains of the black middle class, particularly in *Ebony*, provided evidence for the racial uplift of black folk on a local, national and international scale. By contrast, the endemic problems faced by the South Side's black residents reiterated the importance of Johnson's magazines as an outlet for a community, which continued to be ostracized and ignored.

AN OFFICE AT THE BACK: ENTERPRISE AND EXPANSION ON CHICAGO'S SOUTH SIDE

The roots of Johnson Publishing grew directly out of the fertile ground for black business enterprise provided by the South Side. Johnson started his first magazine *Negro Digest* in a corner office of the Supreme Life Building—home of Supreme Liberty Life Insurance, one of the nation's largest black businesses. At the height of the Great Depression, Johnson had found work for the Company's president Harry Pace following a chance meeting at a local Urban League event.[34] Johnson was assigned to the Company's monthly newspaper, and it was this role, which inspired him to develop *Negro Digest*. He persuaded Earl Dickerson to provide him with a backroom office on the second floor of the Supreme Life building, which became the first address of his publishing enterprise.[35]

In later interviews and his autobiography, Johnson emphasized that *Negro Digest* was both physically and intellectually developed in the space provided by Pace and the unique business atmosphere of the South Side. He noted that Supreme Life had offered him the opportunity "to observe Black people *running* a business. For the first time I believed that success was possible for *me* in business."[36] The public role of the Supreme Life Building—as both the home of one of the nation's most successful black firms and as the "gateway to Bronzeville"—played a key role in this process.[37] Its location at 35th Street and South Parkway was in close proximity to the offices of other black publications including the *Defender* and the *Chicago Bee*.[38] The mutually supportive business environment provided by the Black Metropolis was embodied through Johnson's ability to create a new enterprise from within the Supreme Life offices. By staking his own small claim upon this space, Johnson was able to channel the symbolic value of the building he occupied into a validation of his own publication.

A year after starting *Negro Digest*, Johnson quit his position at Supreme Life to focus on his fledgling publication full-time. With the capital generated from *Negro Digest* he was able to purchase a small storefront office at 5619 South State Street for $4,000.[39] The offices, which were shared with the Beauty Star Cosmetic Company, were just over three miles south of the Supreme Life Building and close to jazz hotspot Club DeLisa and the Coppin Memorial AME Church.[40] Following the introduction of *Ebony* the Company expanded again, leasing a two-story

Figure 6.2.   Restored Supreme Life Building at 35th Street and Martin Luther King Boulevard (formerly South Parkway). Source: Photo by James West, July 2015.

building at 5125 South Calumet Avenue from the South Parkway Community Center. The offices were less than half a mile from the intersection
of 47th Street and South Parkway, which Drake and Cayton had described as the "center of the Black Belt."[41] As Lawrence Patrick Jackson
has noted, these locations cemented Johnson Publishing's place alongside
a range of other black cultural institutions, which were clustered "within
the narrow geography of the South Side."[42]

However, in contrast to the public image of Johnson's periodicals being edited and developed at the center of the Black Metropolis, editor Ben
Burns offers a somewhat different story of the Company's early development. A white journalist and a lapsed Communist, Burns was a somewhat unconventional choice to take the editorial reigns at *Negro Digest*
and subsequently *Ebony*. Burns would later contend that whilst the Company's offices were located at the heart of the Black Metropolis, "for all
practical purposes" much of the early editorial content for *Negro Digest*
and *Ebony* was composed at his home address. This address was situated
in the "lily-white" enclave of South Lake Park Avenue, which was separated from the South's Sides racial enclave by Cottage Grove Avenue,
which functioned as the "arbitrary frontier between black and white
neighborhoods."[43]

Burns's own racial identity, and the fluidity between the personal and
professional spaces he inhabited serves to complicate the public image of
Johnson's magazines as being rooted—both physically and ideologically—within the boundaries of the Black Metropolis. Ironically, Burns was
not only white but was a native Chicagoan. In contrast, Johnson was born
in Arkansas, not born in Chicago, likewise early editors such as North
Dakotan Era Bell Thompson, Tennessean Dan Burley, and South Carolin-
ian Herbert Nipson.[44] His role at the Company may well have influenced
Ebony's early policy of having no by-lines, which can be seen as an attempt to hide the extent of Burns' influence over its copy. This attempt to
obscure the role of Burns within Johnson Publishing can also be seen to
have manifested itself within the Company's offices—the editor suggests
that his own workspace was relegated to a distant corner of the building,
"away from the vision of routine visitors."[45]

Three years later, the Company was once more on the move—this
time four miles north to a renovated funeral parlor at 1820 South Michigan Avenue. The shift to 1820 South Michigan was greeted with a far
greater acclaim in Johnson's magazines than earlier moves.[46] In October
1949 *Ebony* profiled the opening of its new building in a photo-editorial
which purported to "put our offices on display" for readers.[47] Through
offering profiles of individual staff members, and offering "live" photos
of employees engaged in professional activities, the article sought to provide a level of transparency for *Ebony*'s audience that reinforced its
claims to being a representative voice for the black community. Just as
the "Backstage" feature of *Ebony* was frequently used to provide readers

with a glimpse into the "behind-the-scenes activities of a major publishing company," so too was the article on the Company's offices at 1820 South Michigan presenting as an inclusive insight for a trusted audience.[48] Pictures of the editorial staff engaged in lively debate around a boardroom table were accompanied by a description that stressed such gatherings to be "wide-open, give and take affairs with full freedom of discussion."[49]

The civic potential of the building was also emphasized—both through the features of the building itself and the manner of its opening. A prized space was the Company's library, described as one of the best reference sources on black life in the country. *Ebony*'s editors expressed their desire that the library would become "one of the most extensive and thorough in the nation" on matters relating to black culture and history.[50] Another feature noted for its potential value to the public was the building's elegant reception room, which was marked for future exhibits of black photography and art. This performative role as a public space for the black community reflected the broader role of Johnson's magazines in helping to shape the public sphere, and was reinforced by its official opening with two receptions—"one for the press and another for community leaders."[51]

Like previous moves, which had been described as an attempt to secure "more *lebensraum*" for the Company, the relocation was seen as a confirmation of and evidence for the growing reach of Johnson's magazines.[52] The issue of *Ebony* which followed the publication of its photo-editorial on 1820 South Michigan Avenue was announced as the biggest in the magazine's history, and the "largest single regular issue ever published by a Negro magazine."[53] The following month's issue marked the first time the magazine had reached 100 pages, which alongside the opening of the Company's new headquarters was seen to consolidate *Ebony*'s role as the "foremost Negro publication in the world."[54] The connection between the Company's building and the success of its magazines was also picked up by publications such as *Business Week* and *Time*, with particular attention paid to Johnson's own offices.[55] The publisher's "deep buff carpets" and "massive white oak desk flanked by a bronze nude and a gold-painted Dictaphone" reflected his emergence as one of the nation's most prominent black business leaders.[56]

From a different perspective, the politics surrounding the building's purchase would come to play a major role in cementing its position as an ethnocentric location of African American cultural memory. In later accounts of the building's purchase, Johnson contended that when he had initially attempted to buy 1820 South Michigan, he had been rebuffed by white owners who "did not want it known that they were considering selling to Negroes."[57] In an attempt to outwit his racist adversaries, Johnson disguised himself as a janitor for fictional white purchasers. This story offered an amusing account of Johnson's business guile and ingenuity, but also functioned as a broader symbol of resistance against Chicago's systemic housing discrimination and widespread redlining practices. By capitalizing on white prejudicial attitudes, Johnson was able to negotiate the system in a way, which celebrated his business achievements, but also established a rapport with his readers based on the acknowledgement of oppression.

The efforts to situate 1820 South Michigan as a racially unifying space can also be read against its location, which appeared to place the Company outside of the boundaries of the Black Metropolis for the first time. In interviews, Johnson was often quick to stress his continued connection to the South Side through his personal living arrangements in interviews. *Chicago Sun Times* reporter Basil Talbott Jr. noted that away from the Johnson Publishing offices Johnson preferred the comforts of the South Side in an apartment at 845 East Drexel Boulevard, "just five minutes away from his first Chicago home."[58] In his memoirs, the publisher offered a more ambivalent response, contending that State Street and Calumet Avenue were "back streets" and that a move downtown would cement Johnson Publishing as a "first class" enterprise.[59] However, at the time of the move Johnson appeared happy for the building to function not as a confirmation of his desire to integrate his publishing company into the greater business community of Chicago the Black Metropolis but an affirmation of his company's responsibility to black citizens.

This was emphasised by its role as a communal hub for blacks on a local and national scale—within a few years of its opening *Ebony* contended that 1820 South Michigan had been visited by blacks from "every state in the union . . . and at least thirty foreign countries."[60] By the magazine's tenth anniversary in 1955, the building was being described as a "Chicago showplace," which had established itself as a "favorite stopover" for international black celebrities and tourists.[61] Such sentiments were reiterated by external publications such as the *Chicago Daily News*, which noted that the guestbook at the Johnson Publishing offices included the "signatures of visitors from all parts of the world."[62] In turn, the building's educational value was consolidated by the introduction of the *Ebony* Hall of Fame, a "unique historical gallery" comprised of historical documents and memorabilia relating to pioneering black leaders which was housed at 1820 South Michigan and open to the public.[63]

The role of 1820 South Michigan in making race visible was embodied by the neon-lighted *Ebony* sign on its roof, which could be seen "more than a mile away from our office on Chicago's famed Michigan Avenue."[64] One could hardly find a more explicit reminder of the Company's philosophy than a sign which beamed the name of its biggest publication over the Chicago landscape—a name which for Johnson confirmed that "black is and should be a color of high esteem . . . EBONY is a magazine of, by and for Negroes who are proud of their color."[65] However, the sign also symbolized the projection of a particular narrative and representation of black progress and success—one which was not always welcomed by readers and critics of Johnson's publications. Accordingly, the Company's offices became an important public space where individuals and organizations could express dissatisfaction at Johnson's editorial philosophy. This was most clearly expressed through pickets outside the Company's offices. In 1966, a group calling themselves "Concerned Black Women" picketed the building in protest of *Ebony*'s representation of African American women.[66] Several years later a number of black artists utilized the same strategy to highlight concerns that Johnson's magazines were some distance away from being "truly representative of the black community."[67] Headed by militant black poet Don Lee, the protesters "paraded for an hour in front of Johnson Publishing."[68] Such tensions would become more pronounced as the Company planned its most ambitious move yet—to a custom built headquarters one mile further north at 820 South Michigan Avenue.

A POEM IN MARBLE AND GLASS: BUILDING BLACK PRIDE AT 820 SOUTH MICHIGAN AVENUE

In 1972, Johnson Publishing announced the long awaited opening of 820 South Michigan as a "fitting home for the world's largest and most important black periodical."[69] Whilst the politics which surrounded the purchase of 1820 South Michigan had been presented as a victory against continuing patterns of racial discrimination, 820 South Michigan appeared to symbolize the significant gains made by African Americans during the civil rights years and the rise of Chicago's own black community during the years since World War II. During the first great migration, the influx of southern black migrants into Chicago had occurred alongside the city's broader expansion. However, while Chicago's population stagnated during the decades since 1940, the continued influx of Southern black migrants meant the black percentage of the overall population rocketed. By the beginning of the 1970s, Chicago's black population made up over a third of its total residents.[70]

From this perspective, 820 South Michigan was presented not as a further retreat from the Black Metropolis, but as concrete evidence for black Chicago's coming of age. The building's location "midway between our advertisers on the Loop and our readers on the South Side" also served to connect the main body of the Black Metropolis on the South Side with the black dominated enclaves of Garfield Park and Lawndale on the city's West Side.[71] At the building's opening, Johnson claimed that the 820 South Michigan marked a watershed in the struggle for racial equality within Chicago, just as it signaled the true entry of his Company into the publishing mainstream. He described the structure as "a poem in marble and glass which symbolizes our unshakeable faith that the struggles of our forefathers were not in vain."[72] This theme was taken up in local media coverage, which suggested that the building was an instructive example of the broader transformations in American society during the postwar years.[73] Rob Cuscaden of the *Chicago Sun-Times* declared that the building's grand exterior "says—quietly, simply but unequivocally—success."[74]

Connected to this idea was the building's celebration as a bold reclamation of black space within central Chicago, as the first building "built by blacks in Chicago's bustling downtown Loop area since the city's black founder, Jean Baptiste Point DuSable, constructed a log-walled fur trading post beside the Chicago River in 1784."[75] Senior editor Lerone Bennett Jr. took the analogy a step further, arguing that DuSable's trading post and the Company's new headquarters at 820 South Michigan were "linked in time and spirit."[76] In addition, the building reified Johnson's longstanding belief in the city's black exceptionalism and its role as the business capital of black America.[77] It offered a powerful response to the emergence of new black magazines such a *Black Enterprise* and *Essence* which were based in New York. When faced with inquiries over a potential relocation to the East Coast, Johnson contended that Chicago "was not only his home, but also the best 'home' for his publications."[78]

The formal opening of 820 South Michigan was celebrated with an extraordinary full color photo-editorial in the September 1972 issue of *Ebony* which ran across forty pages and was comprised of nearly seventy photographs. Readers were invited into the "headquarters of the world's biggest and best black publication" via a comprehensive floor-by-floor tour which opened up all aspects of the building.[79] Through offering readers such a detailed photographic account of the private offices and work spaces of Johnson Publishing, the photo-editorial stressed the Company's transparency and professional openness. Similarly, by visualizing the magazine's staff in a variety of formal and informal settings, the feature helped to create a sense of public familiarity, and indeed ownership, for the magazine's audience.[80]

This sentiment was reinforced by the building's architectural and aesthetic design. Like the buildings of New York publications such as the *New York Post*, which were promoted "as destinations for the public, not faceless corporate structures," so too was 820 South Michigan presented as an open and inviting space.[81] On the grandest scale, this was seen through the building's sheer concrete and glass facades, and its vast open lobby and reception areas. On a smaller scale, it was apparent through features such as transparent "glass walled" conference rooms.[82] Similarly, the photo-editorial stressed that in many places the building's interior layout diverged from conventional office layouts. *Ebony* announced that instead of creating walled offices, the company favored open-plan work-

Figure 6.3.   Johnson Publishing Company on Michigan Avenue in Chicago.
Source: John H. White, U.S. National Archives and Records Administration, October 1973.

stations for administrative and secretarial employees, which offered "vista views" on each floor.[83]

From a different perspective, 820 South Michigan was clearly intended to fulfill a function beyond its role as a necessary production space by reinforcing the editorial emphasis on black pride and exceptionalism projected by Johnson's magazines. Johnson declared to the *Chicago Tribune* that "as a black person I wanted to build something new . . . it will be a good, symbolic thing for black people."[84] The building was imagined as an insular black world, which provided an environment in which "black creativity could blossom and the production of black magazines could be a joy."[85] This included a cafeteria serving authentic soul food, a black credit union, and lounges stocked with black hair products so that employees could "keep their afros styled."[86] From the role of black architect John Moutoussamy in the building's design to the black florist who cared for the flowers in the building's lobby, 820 South Michigan was represented a key site for black cultural expression and racial solidarity.[87]

In turn, the building expanded on the educational role developed by projects such as the *Ebony* Hall of Fame at 1820 South Michigan. *Ebony* claimed that the building's collection of African and African American art was one of the largest corporate collections of black art in the world. The company hired tour guides and produced a pamphlet tour of the art collection for visitors, which included an index of the artworks on display along with a guide by number, location, and floor.[88] Johnson encouraged readers to stop by and see the artwork for themselves, noting that "we felt it important as there was no one place in Chicago where people could go to see black art."[89] Three years after the opening, Ponchitta Pierce contended that the building continued to be toured by more than five hundred visitors a day.[90] Particular attention was given by the magazine's editors to the visits of schoolchildren, with daily school tours held to both "inspire young blacks and show young whites examples of black people involved in the production of some of the nation's most successful magazines."[91]

A LONG WAY FROM THE SOUTH SIDE: BLACK BUSINESS SUCCESS AND A SECOND GHETTOIZATION OF CHICAGO

However, while the Company's extraordinary efforts to establish 820 South Michigan as a major civic and educational hub for black citizens garnered considerable praise, they did not convince all elements of the magazine's readership. Following the September 1972 photo-editorial, Elaine Armstrong chided the magazine for its "extravagant coverage of your even more extravagant office building." Whilst other readers argued that the new building was "enough to make every black person 'burst at the seams' with pride," Armstrong painted the building as a false idol. She asked *Ebony's* editors how they justified claims that the building was evidence of Johnson Publishing's commitment to black people when "no doubt just blocks away there are thousands of blacks who remain ill-fed, ill-housed and with no chance of ever enjoying the 'fruits' of the nation's wealth."[92]

Such criticisms fed into the words and actions of previous activists such as Don Lee, and reflected persistent criticisms of the Company's editorial biases and class prejudices.[93] Johnson presented his headquarters as "a vehicle for building and projecting the image of black people in America," and as evidence of the gains made by Chicago's black citizens.[94] Yet its extravagance provided a stark contrast with the rise of Chicago's "second ghetto" in the years since World War II. Arnold Hirsch has contended that the city's municipal government and business leaders responded to the continuing influx of black migrants during the 1950s and 1960s not by challenging their ghettoization, but by expanding and reinforcing racial segregation.[95] This entrenchment fostered resentments which burst into life in the aftermath of Martin Luther King Jr.'s assassination in 1968 which left large sections of black neighborhoods on the South and West Side of Chicago in ruins.[96] In 1969 federal district judge Richard B. Austin declared that "existing patterns of racial segregation must be reversed if there is to be a chance of averting the desperately intensifying division of whites and Negroes in Chicago."[97]

Against such problems, the extravagance of 820 South Michigan could be read not as a symbol of black pride, but as further evidence of the company's dislocation from Chicago's black proletariat. This was embodied by Johnson himself, whose outlandish executive suite served as "literally the crowning testimony" to his vast economic success and invited both awe and incredulity in the local press.[98] Spread out across the entire top floor of 820 South Michigan, Johnson's offices included a dining room, an exercise room, a sauna, and its own microclimate system.[99] Patricia Moore of the *Chicago Daily News* recounted the surreal environment which Johnson had created for himself—encapsulated by an image of the publisher working out in his exercise room still dressed in a suit and tie.[100] The journalist also documented the ambivalent reaction visiting students, with Johnson's offices "evoked wisecracks about diamond studded floors after the kids left the building."[101] Another visitor was less subtle, informing the publisher that "now I know what God would have one if he hadn't run out of money."[102]

Johnson contended that the aspirational values embodied by 820 South Michigan, alongside its role in assuming the civic responsibilities of cash-strapped inner city black cultural organizations, offered a powerful vision of racial uplift. *Ebony* drew a direct link between the black middle class and the rise of cultural institutions, asserting that "every major city should have its black art and black history museums and these institutions should be able to depend upon the black middle class for the bulk of their support."[103] However, readers like Armstrong may well have argued that the millions lavished on 820 South Michigan would have had a bigger impact being filtered directly back into South Side Community projects. For all of its focus on black pride, 820 South Michigan can be seen to have celebrated an essentially conservative vision of black entrepreneurial progress that was economically, if not literally, out of the reach of many black citizens.

More broadly, the role of 820 South Michigan as a symbol for black progress—both inside and outside Johnson Publishing Company— served to frame the route to racial advancement in a specific way. Indeed, the presentation of the new Johnson headquarters as a non-threatening challenge and a literally "constructive" response to racially restrictive covenants, must be understood within the context of and in contrast to more "destructive" forms of black urban reaction such as the riots which followed King's assassination.[104] Whilst Eric Easter may have asserted that the building was "its own loud protest," this was a protest quite distinct from, and infinitely preferable to an outpouring of black urban rage for an end to segregation aimed at Chicago's white business district.[105] Relatedly, Hirsch has noted how the ways in which both public and private construction projects helped to entrench segregation on the South Side offered a stark reminder of the "power of private enterprises to shape public policy and the efficacy of violent resistance."[106]

This tension meant that even as some commentators celebrated 820 South Michigan as evidence that Johnson Publishing had come a "long way" from its humble roots in the Black Metropolis, others positioned the building as a marginal and potentially problematic space.[107] In its location "on the periphery of Chicago's Michigan Avenue," the Johnson's headquarters was not truly part of the white business hierarchy which dominated central Chicago, but was also distanced from the city's black proletariat.[108] Similarly, Johnson's claims that he was well aware of the "troubles and frustrations" of many in America's black population did not fully reconcile with his view from his "opulent penthouse office" atop 820 South Michigan.[109] Whilst reporters such as Moore admired the building as a spectacle, they also recognized how its lavish interior could ultimately distract from the continuing challenges faced by black citizens on a local and national scale.[110]

This tension can also be seen through the images of John H. White and other photographers working for the Environmental Protection Agency during the 1970s. At the same moment at which Johnson was celebrating 820 South Michigan as a tool for racial uplift, White was documenting the devastating impact of deindustrialization and urban decay on the city's black population. His images highlighted the limitations of black entrepreneurial success in catalyzing structural change, as Chicago's reputation as the "black business capital of America" appeared to do little to alleviate the endemic poverty and institutionalized segregation on the South Side.[111]

Furthermore, in White's images the Loop appeared as a transitionary space for black citizens, with the Johnson headquarters appearing to confirm not the presence, but the absence of blackness. For all its latent symbolism, 820 South Michigan appears alienated and distant from White's depiction of black life and culture on the South Side.

CONCLUSION

This research has demonstrates how the Johnson Publishing offices became an important part of the company's broader public image which fed into, but also complicated an editorial emphasis on racial uplift and black achievement. Through their popular depiction as important spaces for black cultural production, civic action and racial expression, the different offices of Johnson Publishing looked to consolidate its commitment to black citizens on a local and national scale. In the process, the relationship between the company's offices and its magazines, and the representation of its offices in its magazines, highlighted the intersections between

Figure 6.4. South Side group of black children in Chicago at Playground at 40th and Drexel Boulevard. Source: John H. White, U.S. National Archives and Records Administration, October 1973.

architectural and editorial production, which helped to reinforce an underlying corporate identity and philosophy. The culmination of this role came through the opening of a custom built headquarters at 820 South Michigan Avenue in the 1970s. This site was claimed as a concrete example of black achievement, which paralleled the company's growth with the expansion of Chicago's black population and the broader social transformations in post-war black life. In turn, the building expanded on the previous role of Johnson Publishing's offices as important educational and civic spaces for the black community. Through its extensive art collections and a library which offered thousands of "rare historical books, anthologies, biographies and various other special reference works" on black life and culture, 820 South Michigan positioned itself as a major black cultural institution and tourist attraction.[112]

However, the celebration of the company's new offices, and the lavish nature of their construction and interior design, also stood in contrast to continuing segregation, housing restrictions and racial inequality for many of Chicago's black residents. Just as the emphasis of black achievement and middle-class ideals promoted through *Ebony* and *Jet*'s pages can be seen to have deflected attention away from systemic racial inequalities, the extravagance of 820 South Michigan—and in particular Johnson's executive suite—revealed a disconnect between his magazines and the black community they ostensibly served. From this perspective, the building consolidated the problematic role of previous offices as spaces, which challenged racially restrictive housing covenants and celebrated black enterprise, but also legitimated dominant discourses about acceptable forms of black urban protest and racial uplift.

NOTES

1. St. Clair Drake and Horace R. Cayton, *Black Metropolis: A Study of Negro Life in a Northern City* (New York: Hardcourt, Brace and Company, 1945); Preston H. Smith, *Racial Democracy and the Black Metropolis: Housing Policy in Postwar Chicago* (Minneapolis: University of Minnesota Press, 2012), preface.

2. Drake and Cayton, *Black Metropolis*, 12.

3. Davarian L. Baldwin, *Chicago's New Negroes: Modernity, the Great Migration, and Black Urban Life* (Chapel Hill: University of North Carolina Press, 2007) 25; Christopher Robert Reed, *The Rise of Chicago's Black Metropolis, 1920–1929* (Urbana: University of Illinois Press, 2011), 71–117.

4. John H. Johnson, "Succeeding Against the Odds," *Ebony*, November 1992, 33–34.

5. Adam Green, *Selling the Race: Culture, Community, and Black Chicago, 1940–1955* (Chicago: University of Chicago Press, 2007), 129–140; Noliwe M. Rooks, *Ladies Pages: African American Women's Magazines and the Culture That Made Them* (New Brunswick: Rutgers University Press, 2004), 131–139.

6. Eric Easter, In Memoriam: The Johnson Publishing Building, *The Root*, November 21, 2010, www.theroot.com/articles/culture/2010/11/remembering_the_best_days_of_the_ebony_building.html.

7. William A. Gleason, *Sites Unseen: Architecture, Race, and American Literature* (New York: New York University Press, 2011), 1–3.

8. Lesley Naa Norle Lokko, *White Papers, Black Marks: Architecture, Race, Culture* (Minneapolis: University of Minnesota Press, 2000), 14.

9. Darell Wayne Fields, *Architecture in Black* (London: Athlone Press, 2000); Selden Richardson and Maurice Duke, *Built By Blacks: African American Architecture and Neighborhoods in Richmond* (Charleston: History Press, 2008); Dell Upton and John Michael Vlach, *Common Places: Readings in American Vernacular Architecture* (Athens: University of Georgia Press, 1986); Ellen Weiss, *Robert R. Taylor and Tuskegee: an African American Architect Designs for Booker T. Washington* (Montgomery: NewSouth Books, 2011); Craig L. Wilkins, *The Aesthetics of Equity: Notes on Race, Space, Architecture, and Music* (Minneapolis: University of Minnesota Press, 2007); Dreck Spurlock Wilson ed, *African American Architects: A Biographical Dictionary, 1865–1945* (New York: Routledge, 2004).

10. Bradford Grant, "Accommodation, Resistance and Appropriation in African-American Building" in *Sites of Memory: Perspectives on Architecture and Race*, ed. Craig Barton (New York: Princeton Architectural Press, 2001), 109.

11. Robert M. Adelman and Christopher Mele ed, *Race, Space and Exclusion: Segregation and Beyond in Metropolitan America* (New York: Routledge, 2015); Eric Avila, *The Folklore of the Freeway: Race and Revolt in the Modernist City* (Minneapolis: University of Minnesota Press, 2014); Diane Harris, *Little White Houses: How the Postwar Home Constructed Race in America* (Minneapolis: University of Minnesota Press, 2013); June Manning Thomas and Marsha Ritzdorf, *Urban Planning and the African American Community* (New York: Sage Publications, 1997); Thomas, *Redevelopment and Race: Planning a Finer City in Postwar Detroit* (Detroit: Wayne State University Press, 2013).

12. Caroline Goeser, *Picturing the New Negro: Harlem Renaissance Print Culture and Modern Black Identity* (Lawrence: University Press of Kansas, 2007); Elizabeth Schroeder Schlabach, *Along the Street of Bronzeville: Black Chicago's Literary Landscape* (Urbana: University of Illinois Press, 2013) preface; Stephen C. Tracy, *Writers of the Black Chicago Renaissance* (Urbana: University of Illinois Press, 2011).

13. Maria Balshaw, *Looking For Harlem: Urban Aesthetics in African-American Literature* (Pluto Press, 2000); Barbara J. Bolden, *Urban Rage in Bronzeville: Social Commentary in the Poetry of Gwendolyn Brooks* (Chicago: Third World Press, 1999); Herb Boyd, *Baldwin's Harlem: A Biography of James Baldwin* (New York: Atria Books, 2008); Richard J. Powell ed, *Archibald Motley: Jazz Age Modernist* (Durham: Nasher Museum of Art, 2014).

14. Green, *Selling the Race*, 129.

15. Aurora Wallace, *Media Capital: Architecture and Communications in New York City* (Chicago: University of Illinois Press, 2012), 2–5.

16. Wallace, *Media Capital*, 73; Frederick M. Binder and David M. Reimers, *All The Nations Under Heaven: an Ethnic and Racial History of New York City* (New York: Columbia University Press, 1995).

17. Gleason, *Sites Unseen*.

18. Kevin K. Gaines, *Uplifting the Race: Black Leadership, Politics and Culture in the Twentieth Century* (Chapel Hill: University of North Carolina Press, 1996); Reed, *The Chicago NAACP and the Rise of Black Professional Leadership, 1910–1966* (Bloomington: Indiana University Press, 1997).

19. Baldwin, "Midnight Was Like Day: Strolling Through Archibald Motley's Bronzeville" in Powell ed, *Archibald Motley* 4.

20. Robert M. Silverman, "The Effects of Racism and Racial Discrimination on Minority Business Development: The Case of Black Manufacturers in Chicago's Ethnic Beauty Aids Industry," *Journal of Social History* 31 (1998) 571–597; Commission on Chicago Landmarks, *The Black Metropolis-Bronzeville District: Preliminary Staff Summary of Information* (Chicago: Department of Planning and Development, 1997).

21. Robert Bone and Richard A. Courage, *The Muse in Bronzeville: African American Expression in Chicago 1932–1950* (New Brunswick: Rutgers University Press, 2011) 61–63.

22. Myiti Sengstacke Rice, *Chicago Defender* (Charleston: Arcadia Publishing, 2012), 7–8.

23. Drake and Cayton, *Black Metropolis*, 8.

24. "Backstage" *Ebony*, December 1945, 1; "Backstage" *Ebony*, March 1948, 10.

25. Jonathan Scott Holloway, *Jim Crow Wisdom: Memory and Identity in Black American since 1940*, (Chapel Hill: University of North Carolina Press, 2013), 62-64.

26. "Backstage," *Ebony*, November 1945, 2; Jason Chambers, *Madison Avenue and the Color Line: African Americans in the Advertising Industry* (Philadelphia: University of Pennsylvania Press, 2008), 41.

27. E. Franklin Frazier, *Black Bourgeoisie* (New York: Free Press, 1997), 179; Green, *Selling the Race*, 141–144.

28. John Johnson with Lerone Bennett Jr., *Succeeding Against the Odds* (New York: Warner Books, 1989), 57.

29. James R. Grossman, *Land of Hope: Chicago, Black Southerners, and the Great* Migration (Chicago: University of Chicago Press, 1989), 2–4.

30. Green, *Selling the Race*, 15.

31. Johnson and Bennett, *Succeeding Against the Odds*, 57–65.

32. Robert Bone and Richard A. Courage, *The Muse in Bronzeville* (New Brunswick: Rutgers University Press, 2011), 1.

33. Jeffrey Helgeson, *Crucibles of Black Empowerment: Chicago's Neighborhood Politics from the New Deal to Harold Washington* (Chicago: University of Chicago Press, 2014), 18.

34. Johnson and Bennett, *Succeeding Against the Odds*, 82.

35. Robert B. Pile, *Top Entrepreneurs and Their Businesses*, (Minneapolis: Oliver Press, 1993), 141–142.

36. "Ebony interview with John H. Johnson," *Ebony*, November 1985, 48.

37. Jan Pinkerton and Randolph H. Hudson, *Encyclopedia of the Chicago Literary Renaissance* (New York: Facts On File, 2004), 42.

38. Baldwin, *Chicago's New Negroes*, 33.

39. Johnson and Bennett, *Succeeding Against the Odds*, 133.

40. "Succeeding Against the Odds" Ebony, October 2005, 74D.

41. Drake and Cayton, *Black Metropolis*, 379.

42. Lawrence Patrick Jackson, *The Indignant Generation: A Narrative History of African American Writers* (Princeton: Princeton University Press, 2011), 100.

43. Ben Burns, *Nitty Gritty: A White Editor in Black Journalism* (Jackson: University of Mississippi Press, 1996), 40.

44. "Backstage," *Ebony*, November 1951, 12.

45. Burns, *Nitty Gritty*, 96.

46. "Backstage," *Ebony*, June 1949, 10; "Backstage," Ebony, September 1949, 14; "Welcome To Our New Home," *Negro Digest*, August 1949, 2.

47. "Ebony Opens its New Building," *Ebony*, October 1949, 34.

48. "Backstage," *Ebony*, January 1963, 20.

49. "Ebony Opens Its New Building," *Ebony*, October 1949, 37.

50. "Backstage," *Ebony*, June 1949, 10.

51. "Backstage," *Ebony*, September 1949, 14; C. K. Doreski, *Writing America Black: Race Rhetoric and the Black Public Sphere* (Cambridge: Cambridge University Press, 1998), 92–102.

52. "Backstage," *Ebony*, March 1946, 2.

53. "Backstage," *Ebony*, November 1949, 12.

54. "Backstage," *Ebony*, December 1949, 10.

55. "Ebony: Making a New Market Pay Off," *BusinessWeek*, March 22, 1952, 38. Box 2, Folder 1, Ben Burns Papers, Carter G. Woodson Regional Library, Vivian G. Harsh

Research collection of Afro-American History and Literature, Chicago, IL. June 15, 2015.

56. "Passion With a Purpose" *Time*, October 23, 1950. Box 2, Folder 1, Ben Burns Papers. June 15, 2015; Chambers, *Madison Avenue and the Color Line*, 43–44.

57. Helen Dudar, "The Road to Success" *New York Post*, December 6, 1962. Box 2, Folder 1, Ben Burns Papers. June 15, 2015.

58. Basil Talbott Jr, "Ebony formula the same, only the times change," *Chicago Sun Times*, Box 2, Folder 2, Ben Burns Papers. June 15, 2015.

59. Johnson and Bennett, *Succeeding Against the Odds* 198.

60. "Backstage," *Ebony* (July 1953) 14.

61. "The Story of Ebony" *Ebony*, November 1955, 123.

62. William Kiedaisch, "Chicago Success Story," *Chicago Daily News*, Box 2, Folder 1, Ben Burns Papers. 15 June 2015.

63. "Ebony Hall of Fame" *Ebony*, November 1955, 149–150.

64. "Ebony Opens Its New Building," 34.

65. "Publishers Statement," *Ebony*, February 1946, 2.

66. Evelyn Rodgers, "Is *Ebony* Killing Black Women?" *Liberator*, March 1966, 12–13.

67. "Black Artists Picket Ebony" Box 2, Folder 1, Ben Burns Papers. June 15, 2015.

68. "Ebony Hit For Lack of Militancy," *Washington Post*, December 31, 1969, A2.

69. "Backstage," *Ebony*, September 1972, 22.

70. Helgeson, *Crucibles of Black Empowerment*, 18; Melvin G. Holli and Peter d'A. Jones eds, *Ethnic Chicago* (Grand Rapids: Wm. B. Eerdmans Publishing, 1995), 335.

71. Walter Morrison, "The Long Journey to Wealth," *Chicago Daily News*, August 9, 1973, 5.

72. "New JPC Building Dedicated," *Jet*, June 1, 1972, 16.

73. Morrison, "Ebony: 30 Years of Heritage" *Chicago Daily News*, Box 2, Folder 1, Ben Burns Papers. June 15, 2015.

74. Rob Cuscaden, "Striking Home For Johnson Publishing" *Chicago Sun-Times*, Box 2, Folder 1, Ben Burns Papers. June 15, 2015.

75. "Ebony Magazine's New Home," *Ebony*, September 1972, 94.

76. "New JPC Building Dedicated," 18.

77. Earl G. Graves, "A Double Salute," *Black Enterprise*, June 1974, 4.

78. "Backstage," *Ebony*, February 1971, 26.

79. "Backstage" *Ebony*, August 1972, 30.

80. "Ebony Magazine's New Home," 84–124.

81. Wallace, *Media Capital*, 7.

82. "Ebony Magazine's New Home," 85.

83. "Ebony Magazine's New Home," 110.

84. Lynn Taylor, "Johnson Shows 'Exhibit A'" *Chicago Tribune*, Box 2, Folder 1. Ben Burns Papers. 15 June 2015.

85. "Ebony Magazine's New Home," 102.

86. "Ebony Magazine's New Home," 104.

87. "New JPC Building Dedicated," 10; Frank White, "Black Architects: Shapers of Urban America," *Ebony*, July 1983, 62; David Hartt, *Stray Light* (Chicago: Columbia College Chicago Press, 2013), 61.

88. "JPC Art Collection," Box 15, Folder 20, Hoyt Fuller Papers, Atlanta University Center, Atlanta, GA. June 15, 2015; "Letters to the Editor" *Ebony*, April 1973, 25.

89. "Ebony Magazine's New Home," 104.

90. Ponchitta Pierce, "The Man Who Turned Ebony To Gold," *Reader's Digest*, December 1975, 162.

91. "Backstage," *Ebony*, May 1972, 32.

92. "Letters to the Editor," *Ebony*, December 1972, 24–26.

93. Such criticisms were usually reserved for *Ebony* and *Jet*. *Negro Digest*, which had been cancelled in 1951 but revived in 1961, had been renamed *Black World* and by the beginning of the 1970s had cemented its importance as a major voice for the Black Arts Movement. For more on editorial differences between *Negro Digest* and its more glam-

orous siblings see Abby Arthur Johnson and Ronald Maberry Johnson, *Propaganda and Aesthetics: the Literary Politics of African-American Magazines in the Twentieth Century* (Amherst: University of Massachusetts Press, 1991).

94. "Publishing Company Operated By Blacks Opens New Building," *United Press International*, Box 2, Folder 1, Ben Burns Papers. 15 June 2015.

95. Arnold R. Hirsch, *Making the Second Ghetto: Race and Housing in Chicago, 1940–1960* (Cambridge, UK: Cambridge University Press, 1983).

96. Clay Risen, *A Nation On Fire: America in the Wake of the King Assassination* (Hoboken: John Wiley & Sons, 2009), 141–156.

97. Mary Pattillo, *Black on the Block: the Politics of Race and Class in the City* (Chicago: University of Chicago Press, 2007), 192.

98. Patricia Moore, "Johnson's Office: Ebony Superpad," *Chicago Daily News*, Box 2, Folder 1, Ben Burns Papers. 15 June 2015; Barbara Reynolds, "Johnson Empire Built On One Idea," *Chicago Tribune*, Box 2, Folder 2, Ben Burns Papers. 15 June 2015; Peg Zwecker, "New Office Building A Dream Come True," *Chicago Daily News*, Box 2, Folder 1, Ben Burns Papers. June 15, 2015.

99. "Ebony Magazine's New Home," 120.

100. Moore, "Johnson's Office" Box 2, Folder 1, Ben Burns Papers. June 15, 2015; "Plush Suite For Publisher" *Chicago Daily News*, Box 15, Folder 20, Hoyt Fuller Papers. June 15, 2015; "White Kids in a Black World" *Chicago Daily News*, Box 21, Folder 18, Hoyt Fuller Papers. June 15, 2015.

101. Moore, "White Kids in a Black World," Box 21, Folder 18, Hoyt Fuller Papers. June 15, 2015.

102. Moore, "Johnson's Office," Box 2, Folder 1, Ben Burns Papers. June 15, 2015.

103. "Responsibilities of the Black Middle Class," *Ebony*, August 1973, 180.

104. Janet L. Abu-Lughod, *Race, space, and riots in Chicago, New York, and Los Angeles* (Oxford, UK: Oxford University Press 2007); Fred R. Harris and Roger R. Wilkins, *Quiet Riots: Race and Poverty in the United States* (New York: Pantheon Books, 1988); Kenneth L. Kusmer and Joe W. Trotter, *African American Urban History since World War II* (Chicago: The University of Chicago, 2009).

105. Easter, "In Memoriam: The Johnson Publishing Building."

106. Hirsch, *Making the Second Ghetto*, 255.

107. Rob Cuscaden, "Striking Home For Johnson Publishing" Box 2, Folder 1, Ben Burns Papers. June 15, 2015; Salim Muwakkil, "Will Success Spoil John H. Johnson?" *Black Journalism Review*; Charles Aikens, "Can We Have Liberation and Frivolity at the Same Time?" *Black Journalism Review*, Box 2, Folder 2. Ben Burns Papers. June 15, 2015.

108. Muwakkil, "Will Success Spoil John H. Johnson?" Box 2, Folder 2. Ben Burns Papers. June 15, 2015.

109. Nich Thimmesch, "Ebony Chief Aware of Poverty," Box 2, Folder 2. Ben Burns Papers. June 15, 2015.

110. Moore, "White Kids in a Black World," Box 21, Folder 18, Hoyt Fuller Papers. June 15, 2015.

111. John H. White, "Documerica," *U.S National Archives*, available at: www.flickr.com/photos/usnationalarchives/sets/72157633309290525.

112. "Ebony Magazine's New Home," 110.

SEVEN

From Vivi with Love

Studying the Great Migration

Chamara J. Kwakye

The Great Migration (First and Second Wave) has been recast in the collective American imagination simply as the movement of African Americans from the South to the North and later to the Midwest and West, for better economic opportunities. This recasting in most instances simply footnoting the racialized violence and circumventing any detailed accounts of the terrorism African Americans and other marginalized minorities experienced at the hands of some of their fellow white citizenry, and in many cases exercised by local, state and often federal governments. Recasting the movement of millions of African Americans who endured multiple migrations first out of rural Southern towns to Southern cities and later from Southern cities to Northern, Midwestern, and Western cities for better economic opportunities affirms and solidifies ideas associated with the American Dream and America's Creed. These ideas promote hard work and distort the impact of racialized violence and economic terrorism during that time period. It also diminishes the continued vestiges of slavery and imperialism in the United States. In truth, the movement of millions of African Americans during The Great Migration was a testament to African Americans continued strategies of resistance against the racialized terror that continues to haunt and plague America.

For historians, sociologists and other scholars concerned with studying The Great Migration the approach is often macro interspersed with quotes from individuals, focusing largely on a structural analysis and paying little attention to how structural policies and institutions particularly impacted individuals. In addition much of the scholarly analysis of the Great Migration still focuses on the First Wave migration, 1910–1930. In her remarkable work, *The Warmth of Other Suns*, journalist, Isabel Wilkerson flips this traditional approach on its head and examines the lives of three individuals journey at various times during the Great Migration (2011). Her elegant prose, thorough research and in depth exploration of the impact of the Great Migration through the voice, life and stories of three ordinary, yet remarkable people points to the amazing (historical) work that can be done through personal histories and stories.

In addition, the groundbreaking work, *Southside Girls*, by Marcia Chatelain cannot be overlooked in its contribution to the study of the Great Migration and to Black girlhood. *Southside Girls* centers the stories of Black girls from 1910–1940 during the first wave of the Great Migration and their journeys to and in Chicago, Illinois. Using archives from the Black owned newspaper *The Chicago Defender*, social services institutions and Black philanthropic organizations, Chatelain argues that the construction and meaning of Black girlhood shifted in response to major economic, social, and cultural changes and crises, and that it reflected parents' and community leaders' anxieties about urbanization and its meaning for racial progress. Both Chatelain and Wilkerson's contributions broaden our knowledge of the Great Migration and examine in depth the colossal emotional and physical paradigm shifts of the Great Migration era.

THE GREAT MIGRATION AND BLACK GIRLHOOD

Like Wilkerson and Chatelain, I have devoted much of my time researching, listening to and analyzing the life histories of ordinary remarkable people. In my case much of this early part of my career is devoted to studying the life stories of Black women and girls. In particular, I have been captivated by the stories of Black women in academia. Born of the curiosity of what it's like to be a Black female professor in previous decades, I began thinking about what their day to day lives must be like in the academy and later wondered what led them to pursue the professoriate in the first place. My passion to discover what drives these women, even in the face of what often seems like insurmountable racism and heteropatriarchy,[1] led me to stories about their girlhood. One of the amazing women, Vivi South*,[2] shared not only stories about her girlhood but she also shared the letters she and her grandmother, Nan* had written to each other over fifteen years.

Vivi's family like many African American families during the midtwentieth century had been living in the Southern United States for generations dating back to the Antebellum Period. Vivi, raised by her maternal grandparents, due to her mother's debilitative mental health and her father's absence, was seven years old when she left her grandparent's house in southeast Mississippi with her great aunt (her grandmother's sister) and great uncle for Chicago, Illinois. In all they shared roughly 267 letters, not counting those lost during various moves and those destroyed during a house flood, over fifteen years. It was not until her grandmother Nan passed away in 1978 that she discovered that her grandmother had saved all her letters just as she had.

Their letters tell the story of the Great Migration and allow us to better understand the impact of geography, space and forced/coerced movement on race, class, and sexuality. In addition, the most interesting part of the letters is the view of the Great Migration through the eyes of a Black girl. Their letters not only preserve and denote momentous times in American history, but they also preserve and exemplify the love and refuge created between Black girls and women, even during most extraordinary circumstances and times. Vivi recalls:

> Our letters were our private time, just me and her, Nan and the Special One. I could tell her things in letters that I could never muster the courage to tell her face to face and she could be gentle and kind in ways that she couldn't be face to face, not because she wasn't kind in person, but because she cherished cultivating personal relationships with people. Raising six grandchildren is difficult. Giving each of us our time and showing each of us love separately was very important to her. She had special private relationships with people that were close to her. She made it so she and that other person could live free, take refuge and heal in the relationship she created with them. So I think our letters meant that much more to her because for so long she couldn't do that on a day-to-day basis, in person with me. In one letter she told me that the move robbed her of something she always assumed she "would be able to witness the everydayness" of me. She may not have been able to see the little things like expressions, or me shoot up three inches over a summer, but she got to witness it via the letters, which is why I assumed she saved them. To her my growth, the growth she missed out on was there in those letters.

While the everyday stories and lives of people traversing the Great Migration are understudied, so too are the stories of Black children. Often, children are thought of as resilient or as an afterthought to our larger study of historical moments and even in scholarship that studies contemporary phenomena, the voices of children; the thoughts and opinions of their experiences and contemporary moments are undervalued. Black children and Black girls in particular remain "under voiced." While often the center of many contemporary studies and the targets and victims of policies both historic and contemporary, Black children's voices remain stifled by our preoccupation with saving them. Scholar/artist/activist Ruth Nicole Brown writes,

> Black girls living in their bodies know the all-too-familiar expectations of premature and slow death, as they are often the first to be sacrificed, the expected carriers of heavy loads, made to feel invisible and inferior in spite of a historical legacy that suggests anything but defeat.[3]

Poet and scholar, Nikky Finney writes,

> Black girls know the answers to a wide universe of things but nobody is asking them any questions. We live in a complicated world and Black girls are complex beings. Nobody gives Black girls credit for being complex or for negotiating the height of those complexities.[4]

While scholars across various disciplines (history, english, sociology, gender and women's studies, ethnomusicology, education) are beginning to delve into centering the voices, experiences and the embodied knowledge that Black girls carry within them, often termed as a subfield of Black girlhood studies, we are far from a point of saturation on studying, understanding and sitting with the knowledge of Black girls and Black girlhood. We are just beginning to scratch the surface on what Black girls have to teach us.

WOMANISM AND THE GREAT MIGRATION

The subsequent pages represent not only my attempt to piece together the journey of the second wave of the Great Migration through a Black girl's eyes, but it is my attempt to sit with her experiences and listen to the multiple things she is attempting to know, remember and tell me about race, class and heteropatriarchy in that time period and what her stories inform about those things today. It is also my attempt to ask the reader to do the same and ask them to listen intently to the retelling of these complex encounters told and analyzed by a Black girl.

In addition, equally important to the added historical lessons about The Great Migration and the expansion of Black girlhood studies, the letters between Vivi and Nan presented in this chapter also expand Black feminism,[5] through a Womanist[6] framework. Their letters exemplify the fluid relationship between Womanist theory, Womanist praxis,[7] and Womanist pedagogy.[8] Womanist theory has historically never been separated from praxis and pedagogy, much to the chagrin of Western (Feminist) theorists. This chagrin and misreading of the complexities and nuances of Womanist theory is pointedly explained in literary scholar Barbara Christian's timeless essay, "The Race for Theory."[9] She explains that theory is not foreign to Black girls and women, but a constant. They have, always theorized—but in forms quite different from the Western form of abstract logic . . . our theorizing is often in narrative forms in the stories we create, in riddles and proverbs, in the play in language, since dynamic rather than fixed ideas seem more to our liking. How else have we managed to survive with such spiritedness the assault on our bodies, social institutions, countries, our very humanity? [Black girls and women] continuously speculate about the nature of life through pithy language that unmasked the power relations of their world."[10]

Of Black girls's and women's ability to theorize and produce knowledge Vivi vocalizes,

Long before I was a Black woman in the academy my degrees were conferred, long before I sat in my first undergraduate class, first gradu-ate seminar, I was studying theory, applying theory, testing hypotheses doing fieldwork, conducting ethnographies and doing this (Black femi-nist) work at the close watch of Grandmother, Grandfather, Aunts and Uncles (biological/non-biological), Cousins, neighbors, eye. They were my first teachers. They were the first people I learned to construct knowledge from.

Womanist scholar Layli Maparyan expresses there are five overarching characteristics of womanism: (1) it is antioppression, (2) it is vernacular, (3) it is nonideological, (4) it is communitarian, and (5) it is spiritual-ized.[11] The letters between Vivi and Nan exemplify each of the five char-acteristics of Womanism and vividly represent Black girls and women's ways of theorizing, pedagogy (teaching) and praxis (doing).

The following letters have specifically been chosen as they demon-strate each of the five characteristics of womanism and articulate how African Americans, in particular how Black girls and women survived the Great Migration. The letters have been grouped into three sections: Departures, Defender, and Devotion. Departures contain the letters Nan and Vivi write to each other as Vivi begins her journey north, to Chicago. In Nan's letter, she espouses wisdom that she implores Vivi to keep with her throughout her new journey north, but also in her journey through girlhood into womanhood. Her letter uses Black vernacular and pro-motes education not only as a tool for personal liberation but as a key strategy to decolonization and a key strategy linked to the political prac-tice of service to the Black community. In addition, her letter uses what AnaLouise Keating refers to as *spiritualized politics*. While Nan's letter does allude Christianity in particular, she uses it not as a means to pro-mote an ideal religious dogma, but rather to discuss social-justice acti-vism and perspectives that are informed by spiritual beliefs and prac-tices, rooted in the conviction that spiritual intercession and considera-tion of the transcendental or metaphysical dimension of life enhance and even undergird political action.[12] In addition, in Vivi's letter in Depar-tures, we see a glimpse of the utility and power of extended and fictive kin networks in the African American community. These fictive kin relationships point to the importance of community within a womanist framework as well as the use of vernacular, in particular the importance of Black girls' memory, thoughts and imagination.

This chapter is titled after the Black owned Chicago newspaper, *The Chicago Defender* because of its role in the Great Migration and because of its coverage of Southern lynchings. This section contains the letters between Vivi and Nan and their attempt to make sense of the murder of Emmett Till and state sanctioned violence. Emmett Till's murder happened only months after her arrival in Chicago. As a result Vivi asks of the well-being of her immediate family, but also expresses her fear over the horrific lynching and violence in her home state of Mississippi. In particular, she questions specifically what happened to Emmett Till and why. Vivi's letter points to her clear understanding for the need and a desire for an antioppressive state and points to the stress that racialized violence imposes on the psychic and physical well-being of Black children. Likewise, Nan's attempt to explain Till's murder point to her understanding of the psychic and physical trauma of generational racialized trauma. Nan's explanation also relies heavily on accountability. Vivi's letter clearly asks for an explanation of the state sanctioned violence inflicted on Emmett, a child. While Vivi is not holding Nan accountable for Emmett's death, she is asking Nan to provide her with guidance on how to make sense of a world that can ravage the bodies of Black people. Refusing to rely on the sentiment that children are incapable of understanding the complex nuances of racism and sexism, Nan understands the intellectual, psychological and collective philosophies of Black girl's reasoning. Nan explains to Vivi because she understands the importance of Black girls' questions about the world and the importance of answering them truthfully.

In the final section, Devotion, Vivi and Nan discuss sexuality. Caught between California's 1960s budding sexual liberation movement and the politics of respectability historically used to constrain Black women's sexuality, Vivi formally explains to Nan her disinterest in romantic relationships with men and inertly points to her interest in loving women. Vivi candidly expresses the connection between love, desire, and freedom while also calling out the problems with heteronormativity and freedom. In addition, Nan again uses *spiritualized politics* to frankly critique heteronormativity and to extend antioppression into their conversation of sexuality.

Lastly, following their letters is a brief conclusion of the significance of using womanism to study The Great Migration and its utility of extending further considerations of Black girlhood.

DEPARTURES

Monday, June 6, 1955

My Dearest Special One Vivi,

I'm placing this letter in your suitcase because just like the clothes, shoes, books, barrettes and pressed magnolia flower in between Great Gram MaPe's (my mother, your Great Grandmother Penelope's) bible in it, I want you to keep the words I say to you in this letter close at hand on your new journey. First and always know that the love of God, your family alive and passed on is always with you, providing for you and clearing a path for you. Even when you cannot see it, even when cannot hear it, even when you cannot feel it, God is there, claiming you and moving on your behalf and we are there, the departed are there praying for you, calling your name so that it may forever be in the Lord's ear and carried on the wings of angels. Second, know that your Papa, mother and I only want you to go North with Uncle Cecil and Aunt Lucille because of the many opportunities that you will have there with them and may never have here with us. While I am a proud woman that works hard to care and provide a home with the help, love and work of your Papa, I know too well that my pride and your Papa's pride would wilt like roses in the sun if you were ever to know and meet some of the pain, horrors and danger we and others like us have known to be educated and to survive. And while I know in a world like this there is no way I can ever guarantee your complete and total safety, your Papa and I can guarantee a better chance by allowing you to move North. Third, know that this chance at better comes with a full set of expectations. You have known and heard since before you could read, write and talk the stories about how hard it was for your Papa, Mother and I to be educated. Your Papa learning to read while he was working in the fields, your mother being educated in the best schools and in the private lessons that your Papa and I could afford and me learning to read and write at MaPe's knee's while she worked as a washer woman for a librarian. Our education was hard fought and learned and we always used it to serve our family and our community. Special One, I fully expect the same from you. Let the giving spirit of Christ and community accompany everything you learn. Let everything you learn be in the name of Christ like love. Let everything you learn make you and everyone else free. Learning is sullied if it is not shared. And remember what Papa says, "Learning ain't memorizing the stuff in the books, its knowing in your belly what's between the lines." Keep these lessons about learning close to you as make your way through your schooling. Lastly, know that you are just as God made you, perfect in his sight. That does not mean you will not fail, that does not mean that you will not have shortcomings or obstacles it means that your are whole, despite what anyone else may say, You Are Whole. I fully expect you to write me letters as often as you can. You are an amazing storyteller. You get it from your Papa. So be sure to keep you eyes, ears and heart open and observe everything. I am relying on you to tell me about the world. The family will phone as often as they can and Aunt Lucille and Uncle Cecil's rules are the same as at home. Each morning you must wake up, wash up, make up your bed, get dressed, help with breakfast, eat and get to school on time. Each night you must do evening chores, do your schoolwork, help with dinner, wash up for dinner, eat, read for an hour, listen to the radio for twenty minutes if Aunt Lucille and Uncle Cecil say its okay, take a bath and get ready for bed, lay your clothes out for the next day, pray and then go to bed. You are not on vacation you are at home, just in a different place.

I love you Special One. Always remember that. Keep these words close to you because even if they do not make sense in your seven-year-old spirit and mind now, they soon will.

All my Love,
Nan

Monday, June 6, 1955

Dear Nan,

Thank you for all the surprises in my suitcase. Tell Papa thank you for the fudge from Ms. Early EarlLee. Aunt Lucille is helping me with my spelling for this letter. The ride from our house to the train station seemed like it took forever. Aunt Lucille made me change clothes before we got on the train. Mr. Houston's pick up truck made our clothes very dusty and Aunt Lucille said no respectable folks would board a train anywhere in dust filled clothes. We found a restroom in the train station and changed clothes in there. Aunt Lucille liked my purple dress with the embroidery the best. She said the embroidery was beautiful. I told her I helped you with it. She looked impressesd impressed that I knew how to do embroidery. I told her that I learned from the best. She is wearing a pink suit that she told me used to belong to Great Gram MaPe. It looks just like your powder blue suit, and is almost as beautiful. We are on the train. Nan, there are so many people on the train, White folks and Black Folks. Uncle Cecil's friend Mr. Murray is a porter too. He helped us carry our things and climb the steps to get on the train. His hands look just like Papa's. I was expecting a nickel to pop out of his hands like when Papa does his magic tricks. I asked to sit next to the window. Mr. Murray and Aunt Lucille said I could. I like looking out the window. I like seeing people, and animals and building as we go by on the train. There is a woman sitting near us with skin like Ms. Pearly, soft and brown like pecans she's wearing a yellow dress with white short gloves and big yellow hat that matches. Nan, her hat is beautiful. It looks like the kind Ms. Ethel wore to church on Easter Sunday. I think you would like it. I read your letter. Aunt Lucille helped me read it. I understand some things in your letter. Aunt Lucille told me that she would remind me to read it often until I can remember everything you said on my own. I will be sure to make you, Papa and the family proud with my learning. It is a very long ride to Chicago and Aunt Lucille says I should take a nap. I love you, Nan. Tell everyone I said hello from the train.

Love,
Your Special One,
Vivi

DEFENDERS

Friday, September 2, 1955
Dearest Nan,

Hello from the windy city. (Auntie told me to write that since that's what they call Chicago). I hope this letter finds you in the best of health. I am well and I hope that you and Poppa and J. J., Sara, Tiny, and Phil are well. I miss you all terrible. I started school here in Chicago but Auntie and Uncle said that I will only be in school here until December and then we are moving to California. School is good. There are a lot of new kids in my class. A lot of them moved from the South like we did. I am glad that I'm not the only new kid. They say we talk funny but they're the ones that sound funny to me. How are J. J. and Sara liking school? Do they have Ms. Leeds? She is the best pre-school teacher. I love her. If they do have her tell her I said hello from the windy city or if you see her at church. When you write me back make sure that J. J. and Sara use the back of the paper to scribble a funny birthday note to me. I love them so much. How is Poppa doing without me? Does he miss me? Tell him he owes me a driving lesson for my birthday when I come home to visit. Do you miss me? I miss you and our cooking lessons. Auntie and I canned some peach preserves last week but I don't think they will taste as good as ours. No one's taste as good as the ones we make. How are things in town? Chicago is a big town. I hardly know where we are going most of the time. Uncle says by the time I figure it out it will be time for us to move to California. I hope things are okay in town. I heard Auntie and Uncle and their friends talking about the little boy who was killed in Money, Mississippi. Auntie said it was far away from where we live but it is still in Mississippi where you all live. Nan why did they kill him? Auntie and Uncle said I shouldn't worry about those things but I want to know. He wasn't much older than me. Why would someone kill a child?

Please keep J. J., Sara, Tiny, and Phil safe. I love you so all much. I miss you. Write soon.

   Your special one,
   Vivi

Tuesday, September 13, 1955

My Dearest Special One Vivi,

I hope this letter finds you in the best of health and on the best behavior. Everyone says hello and misses you something terrible. Poppa told me to tell you that he expects you to grow a few inches before you can get that driving lesson. So keep eating your vegetables and drinking your milk. We all plan to call next week for your birthday. I can't believe you are another year older. I'm sure you're shooting up like a weed in the garden. My garden is full of them now that my favorite weed puller is off in Chicago but J. J. and Sara are doing their best to pull the weeds just as good as their big sister. I am glad to hear that you are doing well in Chicago or the Windy City. Remember to carry a scarf and gloves with you at all times, especially as fall draws closer. Auntie called and told me that you were worried about the little boy that got killed. Vivi I don't want you to worry yourself too much but yes the little boy Emmett Till was killed here in Mississippi. Money is quite a ways from here about five and a half hours. I'm not sure why any adult would kill a child but they say that young Emmett was down visiting family from here in Mississippi while on vacation from Chicago. He supposedly got fresh with a young white woman and her husband and another man went and took him while he was sleeping and killed him. I wish I could tell you that this type of thing would never happen again. I wish I could tell you I can always keep you safe from the worlds hate but my dear sweet special one I don't know. Uncle Cecil and Auntie Lucille did not want to tell you about what happened to Emmett because they didn't want you to worry, but I know it is all over Chicago. They probably have talked about it everywhere. Please don't be mad at your Aunt and Uncle. They want just as much as Poppa and I do to shield you from anything that could possibly rob you of the innocence of being a child. Death and the violence that hatred breeds, is not something that we've wanted you to have to deal with but we are ever realistic of the times we are living in. Unfortunately being a black girl child in a world full of hate will always mean that we will have to fight for your innocence and that you will have to grow up faster than the good Lord ever intended you to. Know that I am here for you no matter what and I will always tell you the truth as close as I know it. I know that may not ease your fears but I hope you know that you don't have to be afraid to tell me how you feel ever. I love you special. I must bring this letter to a close but never my love for you.

Praying and loving you always,
Nan

DEVOTION

Tuesday, April 13, 1965
  Dearest Nan,

I hope this letter finds you in the best of health. Nan I don't know what is wrong with me. I have no desire to date boys. None. Auntie and Uncle to some extent have been trying to get me to go out with boys at church and some from school but I don't want to. Some of them are from back home and other places in the South and some are from right here in California. No matter where they're from I'm still not interested. I have nothing against them I just don't feel the way I think most girls my age feel towards boys. My girl friends are all going out on dates and they seem to enjoy themselves. No matter how much they make it sound, I still don't want to go. Is this something I will grow out of? Auntie certainly was hoping it was something I would grow out of. She thinks I'm doing it on purpose, putting off the boy's advances, but I just don't think its right to lead them on. I don't want them expecting anything from me. I don't mind being friends with them but that's all I want to be is friends. I'm writing to you because, Nan you have always been honest with me. What do you think is wrong? I love Poppa and Uncle and I think they're great men. They are what men are supposed to be, loving, caring, kind, thoughtful and strong but I just don't see myself falling in love with a man. I see myself falling in love, just not with a man. Isn't love supposed to be soul stirring? The people that stir my soul are not men, at least not in that way. They are women. I know this isn't my usual letter where I tell you about how things are but I just needed to speak with you flat out. I want to fall in love someday but I want to be free to fall in love with someone that I am attracted to, someone that stirs my soul, that makes me happy, not because they come from a good family or because it's a boy that Auntie and Uncle think have a good solid future a head of them. I hope my words make sense Nan and I hope you will answer back with the truth as you know it as you have always been honest with me. Kiss Poppa for me and tell J. J., Sara, Tiny, Phil and Betty Ann I said hello and that their big sister loves them. If and when you see Lynn tell her I think of her often and I hope she's well. I'll be awaiting your response.
  All my love,
  Vivi

Sunday, April 25, 1965
  My Dearest Special One Vivi,

I hope this letter finds you in the best of health. Poppa, Lynn, Sara, J. J.,
Tiny, Phil, and Betty Ann send their love. I will get right the matter of
your last letter and tell you honestly that there is nothing wrong with you
and on this day the Sabbath I prayed for you. I prayed that God would
give you the foresight to know that despite what your Aunt or anyone
else thinks or claims to know, that you know love is a gift from God. All
God's children need love in order to grow and be whole and free. If you
find love and are called to give it and share it with someone then you
have known what God put us on this earth for. I don't care who you fall
in love with, my only hope is that she recognizes how special and lucky
she is to be in your presence and how blessed she will be if you love her
back. I knew immediately that Poppa was the person that I wanted to be
with. It took him a little while longer to figure that out and lucky for him
I was still around when he figured it out but I have known the love of
God because I have been lucky enough to have shared and have been a
reflection of God's love through my relationship with your grandfather.
My only hope for you Special One is that you develop your ability to hear
God's voice and if you don't hear it that is what I am here for to remind
you to quiet yourself long enough to hear him. You are becoming a
woman and the best thing any woman can do for herself is listen to her
own voice, which is only the voice of God pushing us to be free. Listen to
your voice, follow it and never apologize for loving yourself enough to
listen to your own voice and never apologize for giving the gift of love. I
must bring this letter to a close but never my love for you. I carry you in
my heart always.
  Praying and loving you always,
  Nan

CONCLUSION

Vivi and Nan's letters give is a good look at the power of using a womanist frameworks that address embodied identities associated with race,
gender and sexuality to study the Heartland, Great Migration and memory. However, at the close of this chapter I have more questions than
answers and will seemingly continue to answer them with my ongoing
research on the lives of Black girls and women.

  These questions include asking what can we learn from Black girls. As
the Combahee River Collective wrote in 1977, "If Black women were free,
it would mean that everyone else would have to be free since our freedom would necessitate the destruction of all the systems of oppres-

sion."[13] I wish to extend this sentiment and include Black girls. Racism, sexism and poverty often force Black girls into adult/"womanish" roles well before they are legally recognized as such. Thus, their childhoods are marked with inequality. Black girls are forced to navigate and interpret political spheres, policies, and state institutions from an early age. What we have to learn from Black girls is not only the knowledge they have in traversing systems of domination and oppression, but more notably we should be learning how to move towards freedom from their experiences. What is clear in Vivi's letters to Nan is that even at seven she is theorizing and making clear attempts to practice a freedom that may elude her, but is not beyond her.

Another question that emerges out of this research is how can we use Womanism to deepen our understandings of Black girlhood. Traditionally feminism has approached girlhood with neoliberal empowerment rhetoric; a binary approach that situates adult women as the knowledge holders and girls as empty vessels. In particular its approach has is akin to and relies on the universality western philosophies particularly as they pertain to whiteness, middle class economic status and heterosexuality. Thus further marginalizing queer girls, girls of color, Black girls, and any girls that do not fit into any of the universal notions of girl empowerment from ever being empowered and rendering them even emptier vessels to be filled with western knowledge and cultural expectations. In academic circles, womanism is often assumed to be a(n) (divisive) offshoot of feminism because of its centering of women of color and in particular Black women's embodied knowledge. However, while all womanists are concerned with feminist ideals (the freedom of women from oppression) not all feminists are concerned with womanist ideals, namely, antioppression. Antioppression conveys that womanism is identified with liberationist projects of all sorts. Therefore in its approach to deepening our understanding of Black girlhood, womanism is not invested in replicating an oppressive binary that restricts and strips Black girls of agency for the sake of exalting particular types of Black women. Instead taking a womanist approach to Black girlhood relies on dialogue and building structures of inclusiveness and positive interrelationship for freedom. This fact makes womanism and Black girlhood ideal collaborative space to explore past, present, and future embodied knowledge of Black girls and women.

This and further research is also concerned with how can Black girlhood and womanism expand what we know about the Great Migration. Because Black girlhood is concerned with exploring how Black girls experience and navigate the world and their articulations of freedom and womanism is invested in working with Black girls to destroy the binaries that often help to keep Black girls and women silent then studying the lives of Black girls (now women) that lived through the Great Migration, via archives, fiction or oral history interviews we stand to expand theories of race, class, gender, sexuality, historical youth studies, and organizational theory, across multiple disciplines. Most importantly, we also stand to continue to build on the survival strategies cultivated by Black girls and women for generations.

NOTES

1. Heteropatriarchy is a system of oppression that relies on the universality of white-middle class heterosexual cis-gender men as the center of society. As such all people that fall outside of these categories are seen as abnormal and therefore should be dominated either passively or expressly via laws and policies. For Black a woman in particular, under heteropatriarchy, not only is her labor (physical, intellectual, maternal, etc.) exploited but also the very body she occupies is often relegated as disposable.

2. Vivi South and Nan Lee are pseudonyms.

3. Brown, *Hear Our Truths*, 47.

4. Nikky Finney, "Pinky Swear: SOLHOT & Dr. Ruth Nicole Brown, Pioneer" (Foreword), in *Black Girlhood Celebration: Toward a Hip-Hop Feminist Pedagogy* by Ruth Nicole Brown (New York: Peter Lang Publishing, 2009), xx.

5. Black feminism is the theoretical disposition that Black women face interlocking or intersectional oppression (e.g. class, race, gender) and that these oppressions are inextricable. Thus any movement seeking to eradicate a singular oppression alone does not attend to the intersectional needs of Black women.

6. Womanist framework or womanism centers around Black women and women of colors embodied knowledge and envisions and enacts a world freed from all oppressive structures.

7. Womanist praxis is things done to move all people closer to freedom from all oppression.

8. Womanist pedagogy are the things taught explicitly and implicitly to move all people closer to freedom from all oppression.

9. Barbara Christian, "The Race for Theory," in *Cultural Critique*, no. 6 (Minnesota: University of Minnesota Press): 51–63

10. Barbara Christian, "The Race for Theory," in *The Black Feminist Reader*, eds. Joy James and T. Denean Sharpley-Whiting (Malden: Blackwell Publishers, 2000), 12.

11. Layli Phillips, ed. *The Womanist Reader* (New York: Routledge, 2006), xxiv. Maparyan published this collection as Layli Phillips.

12. AnaLouise Keating, "Shifting Perspectives: Spiritual Activism, Social Transformation, and the Politics of Spirit," in *Entre Mundos/Among Worlds: New Perspectives on Gloria E. Azaldua* ed. AnaLouise Keating New York: Palgrave Macmillan, 2005, 243.

13. The Combahee River Collective, *The Combahee River Collective Statement: Black Feminist Organizing in the Seventies and Eighties* (Albany: Kitchen Table: Women of Color Press, 1986). Named after an 1863 South Carolina military campaign led by Harriet Tubman freeing in seven hundred fifty slaves, The Combahee River Collective (CRC) was a Black feminist lesbian organization that was established in 1974. The CRC was instrumental in highlighting what mainstream white feminist movements were not addressing in terms of the needs of women of color, in particular the needs of Black women. Perhaps most famous is the CRC Statement, which articulates four

critical points and arguments: 1) Genesis of Contemporary Black Feminism 2) What We (CRC) Believe 3) Problems in Organizing Black Feminists 4) Black Feminist Projects and Issues.

Conclusion

DaMaris B. Hill

This research relies on leisure studies, labor histories, oral histories, and newspapers as sites of inquiry for investigating the ways Jim Crow politics and suffrage ideologies intersect. Each chapter helps us to understand the ways "home" is constructed in remembered in regional and national histories. This book is an effort to provide an examination about intersecting narratives pertaining to race and gender oppression. In kind, this book aims to examine the ways in which the collective memory of these intersections informs public histories and present realities.

This book emerges at a time when the United States is experiencing a resurgence of racialized violence and in kind, is suffering from a pervasive amount of patriarchal inequalities branded as democracy. The class/ economic awareness associated with the Occupy Movement that took place a few years before is seemingly forgotten. Racial violence and exploitation dominates the news and media outlets. This book is a means of examining race, gender, and class in the context of environmental memory. This lens serves as a way to look at some of the complexities of the present without ignoring the ways multiple histories inform the space.

The chapters in this collection are in direct conversation with the public dominant narratives expressed in the regional and national histories of the Heartland. It is important to challenge public histories that may be informed by national narratives because these narratives often re-inscribe the social hierarchies associated with patriarchy and marginalization into the American imagination. Whereby, the multiple histories and truths associated with the Heartland space continue to be erased.

This book and the novel I am currently writing were inspired by the feelings of erasure I experienced while living in Kansas. I am particularly grateful for the work of historian Nell Painter; without her studies on exodusters and others, my work would not be possible. Reading *Exodusters* proved comforting to me and served as an example of the ways to expand the public histories of a region.

I am challenging pubic histories, so therefore it is important for me to acknowledge that I am not trained as a historian, nor am I a product of a system of vetting associated with the historical profession. I expect the knowledge and authority associated with this work to be investigated and criticized. Nonetheless, I stand behind this book and the content of historical knowledge within this work. My authority to write such a book comes from my acknowledgement and respect of the literary legacy of black woman creative scholars. My primary profession is that of a poet and writer. Therefore, I am following in the legacy of women poets that have scrutinized our lives, wrestled with our different inheritances of geography, of place; with race, class, sexuality, body, nationality, and belonging, and molded it all into sources of insight and wisdom.[1]

A book that uses environmental memory as a lens is important to me as an African American scholar and writer because I view environmental criticism as being akin to African-based philosophies; ways of knowing and cosmological systems are complex manifestations of the geographies of crossing and dislocation. I consider this theory as one that is an articulation of locatedness, rootedness, and belonging that maps individual and collective relationships.[2] This environmental mental and geographic understanding is present in the African consciousness of the Diaspora. As a product of the African Diaspora, this understanding may have been one of the many contributions of enslaved Africans in the New World. Therefore, it is this complex understanding and African-based awareness of geography that is evident in the cultural imagination of the United States. We can see strains of this philosophy and awareness as articulated in the ways the "wilderness" is featured in the American imagination regarding the frontier, pioneering, westward expansion, space exploration, and others.

NOTES

1. Alexander, Pedagogies of Crossing, 257.
2. Ibid.

Bibliography

1920 Federal Census, Wyandotte County, Kansas, and Jackson County, Missouri. 1920 Federal Census, Wyandotte County, Kansas, and Jackson County, Missouri.

Abu-Lughod, Janet L. *Race, Space, and Riots in Chicago, New York, and Los Angeles.* Oxford: Oxford University Press 2007.

Addams, Jane. *Twenty Years at Hull House.* New York: MacMillan, 1911.

"E. J. Alexander," *Our Land: A History of Lyon County,* Edited by Ted F. McDaniel. Emporia: Lyon County Bicentennial Commission, 1976.

Alexander, M. Jacqui. *Pedagogies of Crossing: Meditations on Feminism, Sexual Politics, Memory, and the Sacred.* Durham, NC: Duke University Press. 2005.

Alamillo, Jose. *Making Lemonade Out of Lemons: Mexican American Labor and Leisure in a California Town, 1880–1960.* Urbana: University of Illinois Press, 2006.

Arredondo, Gabriela. *Mexican Chicago: Race, Identity, and Nation, 1916–1939.* Urbana: University of Illinois Press, 2008.

Baldwin, Davarian. *Chicago's New Negroes: Modernity, The Great Migration, an Black Urban Life.* Chapel Hill: The University of North Carolina Press, 2007.

Barrett-Fox, Jason. "A Rhetorical Recovery: Self-Avowal and Self-Displacement in the Life, Fiction, and Nonfiction of Marcet Haldeman-Julius, 1921–1936." *Rhetoric Review* 21 no.1 (2010): 14–30.

Barton, Craig ed. *Sites of Memory: Perspectives on Architecture and Race.* New York: Princeton Architectural Press, 2001.

Beezley, William. *Judas at the Jockey Club: and Other Episodes of Porfirian Mexico.* Lincoln: University of Nebraska Press, 1987.

Berlin, Ira. *The Making of African America: the Four Great Migrations.* New York: Penguin Books, 2011.

Bissell Brown, Victoria. *The Education of Jane Addams.* Philadelphia: University of Pennsylvania Press, 2003.

"The Black Metropolis-Bronzeville District: Preliminary Staff Summary of Information." *Department of Planning and Development.* Chicago: Commission on Chicago Landmarks, 1997.

Boehm, Lisa K. *Making A Way Out of No Way: African American Women and the Second Great Migration.* Jackson: University Press of Mississippi, 2009.

Bogan, Vicki and William Darity Jr. "Culture and Entrepreneurship? African American and Immigrant Self-Employment in the United States." *Journal of Socio-Economics* 37 (2008): 1999–2019.

Bone, Robert and Richard A. Courage. *The Muse in Bronzeville: African American Expression in Chicago 1932–1950.* New Brunswick, NJ: Rutgers University Press, 2011.

Boyd, Herb. *Baldwin's Harlem: A Biography of James Baldwin.* New York: Atria Books, 2008.

Boyer, Horace Clarence. "Lucie E. Campbell: Composer for the National Baptist Convention." In *We'll Understand it Better By and By: Pioneering African American Gospel Composers*, edited by Bernice Johnson Reagon, 88–108. Washington, DC: Smithsonian Institution Press, 1992.

Brown, Ruth Nicole. *Hear Our Truths: The Creative Potential of Black Girlhood*. Urbana: University of Illinois Press, 2013.

Buell, Lawrence. *The Future of Environmental Criticism: Environmental Crisis and Literary Imagination*. Vol. 52. John Wiley & Sons, 2009.

Bureau of Commerce. 14th Census of the United States. Wyandotte County, Kansas, 1920.

Bureau of Commerce. 14th Census of the United States. Jackson County, Missouri, 1920.

Burns, Ben. *Nitty Gritty: A White Editor in Black Journalism*. Jackson: University Press of Mississippi, 1996.

"Can't Stop the Ku Klux Klan," *Emporia Gazette* July 25, 1921. Kansas Memory. www.kansasmemory.org/item/214409

Chalmers, David. *Hooded Americanism*. Durham, NC: Duke University Press, 1987.

Chambers, Jason. *Madison Avenue and the Color Line: African Americans in the Advertising Industry*. Philadelphia: University of Pennsylvania Press, 2008.

Chatelain, Marcia. *Southside Girls: Growing Up in the Great Migration*. Durham, NC: Duke University Press, 2015.

Christian, Barbara. "The Race For Theory." In *The Black Feminist Reader*, edited by Joy James and T. Denean Sharpley-Whiting. Malden, MA: Blackwell Publishers, 2000.

Collier, John. "Blacks and Emporia," In *Our Land: A History of Lyon County*, edited by Ted F. McDaniel. Emporia, KS: Lyon County Bicentennial Commission, 1976

Collins, Patricia Hill. *Black Feminist Thought*: Knowledge, Consciousness, and the Politics of Empowerment . Boston: Unwin Hyman, 1990.

The Combahee River Collective. *The Combahee River Collective Statement: Black Feminist Organizing in the Seventies and Eighties*. Albany, NY: Kitchen Table: Women of Color Press, 1986.

Cuscaden, Rob. "Striking home for Johnson Publishing." *Chicago Sun Times*, May 14, 1972.

Dahl, Linda. *Morning Glory: A Biography of Mary Lou Williams*. New York: Pantheon Books, 1999.

Davis, Angela Y. *Blues Legacies and Black Feminism: Gertrude "Ma" Rainey, Bessie Smith and Billie Holiday*. New York: Pantheon Books, 1998.

Dickerson, James. *Just for a Thrill: Lil Hardin Armstrong, First Lady of Jazz*. New York: Cooper Square Press, 2002.

"DOCUMERICA: Images of America in Crisis in the 1970s." *The Atlantic*, November 16, www.theatlantic.com/infocus/2011/11/documerica-images-of-america-in-crisis-in-the-1970s/100190.

"DOCUMERICA: John H. White," *U.S. National Archives*. www.flickr.com/photos/us-nationalarchives/sets/72157633309290525.

Driggs, Frank and Chuck Haddix. *Kansas City Jazz: From Ragtime to Bebop—A History*. Oxford, UK: Oxford University Press, 2005.

Driggs, Frank."My Story by Andy Kirk as Told to Frank Driggs," *The Jazz Review* vol 2, 1959.

Dudar, Helen. "The Road to Success." *New York Post*, December 7, 1962, 53.

Ellis, Roy. *A Civic History of Kansas City, Missouri*. Springfield, MO: Elkins-Swyers Company, 1930.

Emporia Gazette. Emporia, KS: December 9, 1947.

Fernett, Gene. *Swing Out: Great Negro Dance Bands*. Midland, MI: The Pendell Company, 1970.

Finney, Nikky. Foreword to *Black Girlhood Celebration: Toward a Hip-Hop Feminist Pedagogy* by Ruth Nicole Brown. New York: Peter Lang Publishing, 2009, xiii–xxii.

Fogarty, Robert S. *All Things New: American Communes and Utopian Movements, 1860–1914.* Lanham, MD: Lexington Books, 2003.

Gagliardo, Dominico. "The Gompers-Allen Debate on the Kansas Industrial Court." *Kansas History* 3 no.4 (1934): 385–395.

Galton, Francis, "Eugenices: Its Definiton, Scope, and Aims." *The American Journal of Sociology 10*, no. 1 (July, 1904): 1.

Easter, Eric. "In Memoriam: The Johnson Publishing Building." *The Root*, November 21, 2010, www.theroot.com/views/memoriam-johnson-publishing-building.

El Cosmopolita May 22, 1915

Fur, Gunlog. *A Nation of Women: Gender and Colonial Encounters Among the Delaware Indians.* University of Pennsylvania Press, 2012.

Galarza, Ernesto. *Barrio Boy.* New York: Ballantine Books, 1971.

Gann, Dustin. "Written in Black and White: Creating an Ideal America, 1919–1970." PhD dis, University of Kansas, 2012. Print.

García, José. *History of Mexicans in Topeka, 1906–1966*, manuscript, Topeka Public Library.

Glancy, Diane. *It Was Then.* Lawrence, KS: Mammoth Publications, 2012.

Gleason, William A. *Sites Unseen: Architecture, Race, and American Literature.* New York: New York University Press, 2011.

Gledhill, John. *Neoliberalism, Transnationalism, and Rural Poverty: A Case Study of Michoacán, Mexico.* Boulder, CO: Westview Press, 1995.

Green, Adam. *Selling the Race: Culture, Community and Black Chicago, 1940-1955.* Chicago: University of Chicago Press, 2007.

Gross, Kali N. *Colored Amazons: Crime, Violence, and Black Women in the City of Brotherly Love, 1880–1910.* Durham, NC: Duke University Press, 2006.

Grossman, James R. *Land of Hope: Chicago, Black Southerners, and the Great Migration.* Chicago: University of Chicago Press, 1989.

———."Blowing the Trumpet: The "Chicago Defender" and Black Migration during World War I." *Illinois Historical Journal* 78 (1985): 82–96.

Guadalupe Center Collection. Special Collections. Missouri Valley Room. Kansas City, Missouri Public Library.

Haldeman-Julius, Emanuel. *The First Hundred Million.* New York: Simon and Schuster, 1928.

Haldeman-Julius, Marcet. *Talks with Joseph McCabe and Other Confidential Sketches.* Girard, KS: Haldeman-Julius Publishing Company, 1931.

———. "What the Negro Students in Kansas Endure." *The Haldeman-Julius Monthly* 7 no.2 (1928): 5-16, 147–159.

———. Letter to James Weldon Johnson. October 12, 1927.

Harris, Diane S. *Little White Houses: How the Postwar Home Constructed Race in America.* Minneapolis: University of Minnesota Press, 2013.

Harris, Fred R and Roger R. Wilkins. *Quiet Riots: Race and Poverty in the United States.* New York: Pantheon Books, 1988.

Harrison, Daphne Duval. *Black Pearls: Blues Queens of the 1920s.* New Jersey: Rutgers University Press, 1998.

Hayden, Dolores. *The Power of Place: Urban Landscapes as Public History.* Cambridge, MA: The MIT Press, 1997.

Henderson, Mae Gwendolyn. Speaking in Tongues: Dialogics and Dialectics and The Black Woman Writer's Literary Tradition," *Reading black reading feminist: a critical anthology* Edited by Henry Louis Gates, Jr. (New York: Meridian, 1990), 116–144.

Hirsch, Arnold R. *Making the Second Ghetto: Race and Housing in Chicago, 1940–1960.* Cambridge: Cambridge University Press, 1983.

Hobshawn, Eric. *The Jazz Scene.* New York: Pantheon Books, 1993.

———. "The Invention of Tradition." In *The Invention of Tradition*, edited by Eric Hobsbawm and Terrence Ranger. Cambridge, UK: Cambridge University Press, 1983.

hooks, bell. *Feminism is for everybody: Passionate politics.* Chicago: Pluto Press, 2000.

Huntington, Samuel P. *American Politics: The Promise of Disharmony*. Cambridge, MA: Harvard University Press, 1981.

Innis-Jimenez, Michael. *Steel Barrio: the Great Mexican Migration to South Chicago, 1915–1940*. New York: New York University Press, 2013.

Johnson, John H. with Lerone Bennett Jr. *Succeeding Against the Odds*. New York: Warner Books, 1989.

Jones, Lila Lee. "The Ku Klux Klan in Eastern Kansas During the 1920s" MA thes. Emporia Kansas State College, 1975.

Jordan, Herbert W. "A Klan Cross on Main Street Follows Speech," *Topeka Daily Capital* (Topeka, KS), Sept. 23, 1924. *Kansas Memory*, accessed June 19, 2014. www.kshs.org/p/william-allen-white-s-1924-gubernatorial-campaign/13257.

Kansas State Census, Wyandotte County, Kansas, 1915; Bureau of Commerce, 14th Census of the United States, Wyandotte County, Kansas and Jackson County, Missouri, 1920.

Keating, AnaLouise. "Shifting Perspectives: Spiritual Activism, Social Transformation, and the Politics of Spirit." In *Entre Mundos/Among Worlds: New Perspectives on Gloria E. Azaldua*, edited by AnaLouise Keating. New York: Palgrave Macmillan, 2005. 241–254.

Kernodle, Tammy. *Soul on Soul: The Life and Music of Mary Lou Williams*. Boston: Northeastern University Press, 2004.

———. "Having Her Say: The Blues as the Black Woman's Lament." In *Women's Voices Across Musical Worlds*, edited by Jane A. Bernstein, 213–231. Boston: Northeastern University Press, 2004.

Kirk, Andy and Lee, Amy. *Twenty Years on Wheels*. Ann Arbor, MI: The University of Michigan Press, 1989.

Kirk, Gordon W., and Herbert David Croly. *The Promise of American Life*. East Lansing: Michigan State University, 1914.

Kufrin, Joan and George. *Uncommon Women*. Piscataway, NJ: New Century Publishers, Inc., 1981.

Kusmer, Kenneth L and Joe W. Trotter. *African American Urban History since World War II*. Chicago: The University of Chicago, 2009.

Laird, Judith Fincher. "Argentine, Kansas: the Evolution of a Mexican-American Community, 1905–1940." PhD dissertation. University of Kansas, 1975.

Lindley, E. H. Letter to Marcet Haldeman-Julius. September 30, 1927.

López, Domingo. "La Yarda," *Fiesta Mexicana 1988: 55th Anniversary* Topeka, Kansas: Our Lady of Guadalupe Parish, 1988.

Mays, Ben E. "Real Black Pride." *Chicago Defender*. June 4, 1977: 15.

Mendoza, Valerie. "The Creation of a Mexican Immigrant Community in Kansas City, 1890–1930," PhD diss., University of California, Berkeley, 1997.

———. "Creation of a Mexican Immigrant Community" and Mendoza, "Policing Gender: Mexicans and the American Legal System, the Case of Kansas City, 1910–1940," forthcoming.

Mines, Cynthia. "Riding the Rails to Kansas," PhD diss.,University of Kansas, 1980.

Miller, Loren. "The Unrest among Negro Students at a White College: The University of Kansas." *The Crisis* 34 (1927): 187–188.

Momaday, Scott. *The Man Made of Words*. New York: St. Martins Griffin, 1997.

Morrison, Walter. "Ebony: 30 years of heritage." *Chicago Daily News*, October 29, 1975. 5.

Moursouris, Melissa. "Mary Lou Williams: Musicians as Healer." *Village Voice* 24, July 23, 1979.

Norle Lokko, Lesley N. *White Papers, Black Marks: Architecture, Race, Culture*. Minneapolis: University of Minnesota Press, 2000.

Oppenheimer, Robert. Interviews. Kenneth Spencer Research Library. University of Kansas.

Oppenheimer, Robert. "Acculturation or Assimilation: Mexican Immigrants in Kansas, 1900 to World War II." *Western Historical Quarterly* 16, 1985.

Orsi, Robert. *Madonna of 115th Street: Faith and Community in Italian Harlem, 1880–1940*. New Haven, CT: Yale University Press, 1985.

———. *Thank You St. Jude: Women's Devotion to the Patron Saint of Hopeless Causes*. New Haven, CT: Yale University Press, 1996.

Page, Clarence. "Powerful Positive Thinker." *Chicago Tribune*, April 30, 1989.

Painter, Nell I. *Exodusters: Black Migration to Kansas After Reconstruction*. New York: Knopf, 1976.

Pearson, Nathan W. Jr. *Goin' to Kansas City*. Chicago: University of Chicago Press, 1994.

Pleck, Elizabeth. *Celebrating the Family: Ethnicity, Consumer Culture, and Family Rituals*. Cambridge, MA: Harvard University Press, 2000.

Polk's Kansas City, Kansas Directory 1915. Kansas City, MO: Gate City Directory Company, 1915.

Polk's Kansas City, Kansas Directory 1925. Kansas City, MO: Gate City Directory Company, 1925.

Polk's Kansas City, Kansas City Directory 1929. Kansas City, MO: Gate City Directory Company, 1929.

"Population of the 100 largest urban places: 1910." *United States Census Bureau*. www.census.gov/population/www/documentation/twps0027/tab14.txt.

"Portrait of Black Chicago." *National Archives*. www.archives.gov/exhibits/portrait_of_black_chicago/introduction.html.

Roberts, Dorothy. *Killing the Black Body*. New York: Pantheon, 1997.

Said, Edward W. "Invention, memory, and place." *Critical inquiry* (2000): 175–192.

———. *Orientalism*, (New York: Vintage Books, 1978),

Sánchez, George. *Becoming Mexican American: Ethnicity, Culture, and Identity in Chicano Los Angeles, 1900–1945*. Oxford: Oxford University Press, 1993.

Schwieder, Dorothy, Joseph Hraba, and Elmer Schwieder. *Buxton: a Black Utopia in the Heartland*. Iowa City: University of Iowa Press, 2003.

Schoener, Allon. *Harlem on My Mind: Cultural Capital of Black America, 1900–1968*. New York: Random House, 1969.

Sharratt, Mary. "Time Passages: The Year's Best Historical Fiction" *NPR Books*. NPR. December 6, 2012. Web. August 31, www.npr.org/2012/12/06/166481809/time-passages-the-years-best-historical-fiction.

Shaw, Stephanie, J. *What a Woman Ought to Be and to Do: Black Professional Women Workers During the Jim Crow Era*. Chicago: University of Chicago Press, 1996.

Silverman, Robert M. "The Effects of Racism and Racial Discrimination on Minority Business Development: The Case of Black Manufacturers in Chicago's Ethnic Beauty Aids Industry." *Journal of Social History* 31 (1998): 571–597.

Sloane, Charles Wilson. "Kansas Battles the Invisible Empire: The Legal Ouster of the KKK from Kanas, 1922–1927." *Kansas Historical Quarterly*. 40.3 (1974): 393–409. Print.

Smith, Michael M. "The Mexican Immigrant Press Beyond the Borderlands: the Case of El Cosmopolita, 1914–1919." *Great Plains Quarterly* (Spring 1990).

Smith, Preston H. *Racial Democracy and the Black Metropolis: Housing Policy in Postwar Chicago*. Minneapolis: University of Minnesota Press, 2012.

Spiegel, Gabrielle M. "History, Historicism, and the Social Logic of the Text in the Middle Ages." *Speculum* 65 (1990): 59–86.

———. "Memory and history: Liturgical Time and Historical Time." *History and Theory* 41 no.2 (2002): 149–162.

———. *The Past as Text: The Theory and Practice of Medieval Historiography*. Baltimore, MD: Johns Hopkins University Press, 1999.

———. *Practicing History: New Directions in Historical Writing After the Linguistic Turn*. New York: Routledge, 2004.

St. Clair Drake, John G. and Horace R. Cayton. *Black Metropolis: A Study of Negro Life in a Northern City*. Chicago: University of Chicago Press, 1993.

Strong, H. A. "Bunkum Bill White and Other Bunk." *The Independent,* September 26, 1924: 7.

Strong, Orin. "Klan Christianity." *The Independent,* August 22, 1924: 5.

———. "Kindly Soul." *The Independent,* March 5, 1926: 1.

———. "The Women Folks." *The Independent* August 29, 1924: 2.

———. "The Blue Books." *The Independent* February 12, 1926: 1.

———. "Dynamiting Religion." *The Independent* May 7, 1926: 1.

———. "Married Again!" *The Independent* May 14, 1926: 2.

Stowe, David W. "Jazz in the West: Cultural Frontier and Region during the Swing Era." *The Western Historical Quarterly* 23, no. 1 (Feb. 1992): 53–73.

Sutton, Robert. *Heartland Utopias.* DeKalb, IL: Northern Illinois University Press. 2009.

Talbott Jr, Basil. "Ebony formula the same, only the times change." *Chicago Sun Times,* November 21, 1965: 52.

Taylor, Lynn. "Johnson Shows 'Exhibit A.'" *Chicago Tribune,* May 17, 1972.

Teddy Roosevelt's New Nationalism. www.heritage.org/initiatives/first-principles/primary-sources/teddy-roosevelts-new-nationalism.

"The Kansas Challenge to Unionism." *The New Republic,* June 1, 1921: 3–5.

Trowbridge, William. *Put This On, Please: New and Selected Poems.* Pasadena, CA: Red Hen Press, 2014.

Tuttle, William. "Separate but Not Equal: African Americans and the 100-year Struggle for Equality in Lawrence and at the University of Kansas, 1850s-1960." In *Embattled Lawrence,* edited by Dennis Domer and Barbara Watkins, 139–151. Lawrence: University of Kansas Press, 1988.

Unterbrink, Mary. *Jazz Women at the Keyboard.* Jefferson, NC: McFarland and Co. Publishers, 1983.

Upton Sinclair, *The Jungle.* Second edition. New York: Dover, 2001. First published 1906 by Doubleday.

U.S. Census Bureau, Wyandotte County, Kansas and Jackson County, Missouri. Issued 1920.

Vincent, Ted. "The Community that Gave Jazz to Chicago." *Black Music Research Journal* 12, no. 1 (Spring 1992): 43–55.

Wade M. Cole. *Uncommon Schools: The Global Rise of Postsecondary Institutions for Indigenous Peoples.* Stanford, CA: Stanford University Press, 2011.

Wallace, Aurora. *Media Capital: Architecture and Communications in New York City.* Chicago: University of Illinois Press, 2012.

Walker, Alice. *In Search of Our Mothers' Gardens: Womanist Prose.* New York: Harcourt, Inc., 1983.

White, William Allen. Quoted in the *Topeka Daily Capital,* September 23, 1924. *Kansas Memory.* Accessed June 19, 2014. www.kansasmemory.org/item/214412.

Wiese, Andrew ed. *Places of Their Own: African American Suburbanization in the Twentieth Century.* Chicago: University of Chicago Press, 2004.

Williams, Martin. "Jazz: What Happened in Kansas City?" *American Music* 3, no. 2 (Summer 1989): 171–179.

Williams, Mary Lou. "Mary Lou on the Clouds of Joy." *Melody Maker* 30 (April 17, 1954): 5.

———. "Mr. 5x5 Had a Ten Block Voice." Melody Maker 30 (April 24, 1954): 5.

Wilkerson, Isabel. *The Warmth of Other Suns: the Epic Story of America's Great Migration.* New York: Random House, 2010.

Wilkins, Craig L. *The Aesthetics of Equity: Notes on Race, Space, Architecture, and Music.* Minneapolis: University of Minnesota Press, 2007.

Wilson, John. *Mary Lou Williams Oral History Interview. The National Endowment of the Arts/Institute of Jazz Studies,* 1977.

Wilson, Matthew W. and Sarah Elwood "Capturing," *The SAGE Handbook of Human Geography, 2v,* edited by Roger Lee, Noel Castree, Rob Kitchin, Vicky Lawson, Anssi Paasi, Chris Philo, Sarah Radcliffe, Susan M. Roberts, Charles Withers.

Yanow, Scott. "Julia Lee," www.allmusic.com/artist/julia-lee">http://www.allmusic.com/artist/julia-leemn0000255753/biography. Accessed July 7, 2014.

Zwecker, Peg. "New Office Building a Dream Come True." *Chicago Daily News*, May 17, 1972, 37.

Index

Acosta, Luis, 38
Addams, Jane, 69, 72–74, 76, 79
African Americans: black leisure industry, 10, 45–61; Kansas as "free state", 5, 7, 8; as Ku Klux Klan target, 24; lynchings, 55, 79, 110; mass exodus from Tennessee, 7; as servile labor,. *See also* slavery 22; women as musicians, 45–46, 50–60; Black feminism; Black girlhood
African Diaspora, 122
Alexander, Edward Jones, 24
Allen, Forrest C. "Phog", 75–76, 78
Allen, Henry, 66–68, 73, 79
Alphonso Trent Orchestras, 49
American Association of University Presidents, 75
American Creed, 1–2, 4, 7, 8, 20n8, 105; assimilation in, 7; basis of, 2; conflict with democracy, 23; eugenic science and, 6–7, 10, 11; Heartland as manifestation of, 2, 4; intersection with embodied histories, 2, 22; utopian ideals and, 3–6. *See also* American Dream
American Dream,. *See also* American Creed 4, 8, 11, 70, 105
Andy Kirk's Twelve Clouds of Joy, 50, 55, 56, 58, 60, 61
Anglo-American ethnic identity, 6, 7
The Appeal to Reason (socialist weekly), 69, 72, 81n15
Armstrong, Elaine, 96–98
Armstrong, Lil Hardin, 45
Armstrong, Louis, 45, 85
Austin, Lovie, 45, 53
Austin, Richard B., 97

Baker, Amos, 78
Baldwin, Davarian, 10, 48

Baldwin, James, 85
Barrett-Fox, Jason, 10, 65–79
baseball: and Mexican Americans, 38, 43n67; Negro Baseball League, 50, 63n11
Basie, Count, 58
Beauty Star Cosmetic Company (Chicago), 89
Bell, Alexander Graham, 6
Bennett, Lerone, Jr., 94
Ben Smith's Blue Syncopators, 49
Berger, Victor, 69
Birth of a Nation (film), 66, 69
Black Enterprise, 94
Black feminism: nature of, 118n5; womanism as type of, 21
Black girlhood: embodied knowledge of black girls, 108, 116, 117; in the Great Migration, 105–107; Nan Lee (pseudonym), 106–117; Vivi South (pseudoym), 11, 106–107, 108–117; womanism and Great Migration, 108–110, 117
Black Metropolis (Drake and Cayton), 83, 86–89, 92, 93, 98
Black Nationalist Movement, 1
blacks. *See* African Americans
Black Swan (label), 46, 48, 61
"Bleeding Kansas", 79
blues, 46–49, 51–53, 56, 58
"Blues Clarinet Stomp", 58
boogie woogie, 55, 56, 58
Bowes, Lillian, 48
boys and men. *See* men and boys
Bronzeville (Chicago), 83–84, 85, 88
Brooks, Gwendolyn, 85
Brown, John, 5
Brown, Piney, 50
Brown, Ruth Nicole, 107–108
Brown v. Board of Education, 79

134   *Index*

Haldeman-Julius, Marcet, 10, 68–74, 76,
   78, 79; background of, 69; influence
   of Jane Addams, 69, 72, 73–74, 76,
   79; institutional racism at the
   University of Kansas, 74–79;
   opposition to segregation, 71, 72;
   reform work of, 72–74
Haldeman-Julius Publishing
   Company, 68–79; *The Appeal to
   Reason* (socialist weekly), 69, 72,
   81n15; *Haldeman-Julius Monthly*, 76;
   Haldeman-Julius Weekly, 70; *The
   Independent* (Crawford County,
   Kansas) versus, 67, 68–74, 75, 79;
   Little Blue Books, 68, 71, 74, 76
Hall, Stanley, 75, 76
Handy, W. C., 47
Hardin, Lil, 53
Harlem Renaissance, 85
Harris, Diane, 85
Hawkins, Coleman, 60
Heartland: anti-immigrant sentiments
   in, 6; challenging public histories of,
   121; collective memories of, 2, 3, 5;
   economic collapse of, 1;
   ethnocentricity of, 7, 8; eugenic
   campaigns, 6–7, 10, 11; as
   geographic space, 2; as "imagined
   geography", 3; immigrant groups,.
   See also African Americans; Mexican
   Americans 4, 5, 7, 9–10, 67, 70; jazz
   evolution in, 47–49, 51–52, 58, 61;
   Latina communities, 9, 32, 36,
   41n25; Lenape/Delaware Indians, 9,
   19; as manifestation of American
   Creed, 2, 4; mass migrations of
   nineteenth century, 4, 11; nature of,
   3; population diversity, 4, 5, 7, 8–10,
   48; utopian ideals and, 3, 4, 7, 11
Heartland Utopias (Sutton), 6, 7
Henderson, Mae G., 20n2, 21
Hendricks, Wanda, 8
Heteropatriarchy, 118n1
Hidalgo, Miguel, 37
Hill, Damaris B., 1–11, 21–23
Hines, Earl, 58
Hirsch, Arnold, 97, 98
Hobsbawm, Eric, 40n13
Holmes, Winston, 52

home: construction in regional and
   national histories, 121; embodied
   history and, 22; environmental
   memory of Johnson Publishing
   Company, 10; Heartland Migration
   and, 11; histories rooted in body
   and, 22; Johnson Publishing
   Company locations in Chicago, 10,
   83–100; Latina communities in
   shaping, 9, 32, 36, 41n25; Lenape/
   Delaware loss of homeland, 22, 23;
   origins of justice in, 73
hooks, bell, 23
Howard, Jack, 58
Hull House, 69

The Illinois Miner, 68
"Imagined geography/imaginative
   geography" (Said), 12n9
The Independent (Crawford County,
   Kansas), 67, 68–74, 75, 79
Independent Party, 24
Indian Wars, 24
Indigenous Americans: assimilation
   into mainstream society, 22, 23;
   collective memory of, 23; genocide
   of, 22; as Ku Klux Klan target, 24;
   land in the Heartland, 22, 23;
   Lenape/Delaware Indians, 9, 19;
   male support for females, 19, 23;
   power of language and, 23–24; tribal
   sovereignty, 22
industrial revolution, 4
In Search of Our Mothers' Gardens
   (Walker), 20n1
intersectional identity: collective
   memory and, 8; leisure industry
   and, 8, 10; simultaneous discourses
   and, 21; Suffrage and Jim Crow, 10,
   22, 70
Invented tradition (Hobsbawm), 40n13

Jackson, Lawrence Patrick, 89
Jackson, Marion, 58
Jaime, Nicolás, 36
James, William, 75, 76, 77
jazz: black female performers, 45–46,
   50–60; evolution in the Heartland,
   47–49, 51–52, 58, 61; gender

About the Editor and Contributors

About the Editor

DaMaris B. Hill is an assistant professor of African American and Africana studies and creative writing at the University of Kentucky. She completed her graduate studies at the University of Kansas earning terminal degrees in english, creative writing and women, gender, and sexuality studies. Similar to her creative process, Dr. Hill's scholarly research is interdisciplinary and examines the intersections between literary criticism, cultural studies, and digital humanities.

About the Contributors

Jason Barrett-Fox is an assistant professor of English at Arkansas State University. He received his PhD in English from the University of Kansas. His research interests center around rhetorical historiography, public rhetoric, feminist, engendered and embodied rhetorics, public rhetorics, and alternative and indirect rhetorics.

Tammy L. Kernodle, a specialist in African American music and gender studies in music, is professor of musicology at Miami University (OH). She received her bachelor's degree in choral music education from Virginia State University and did her graduate work in music history at The Ohio State University, where she received a MA and PhD in 1993 and 1997 respectively. Her teaching and research has focused on many different genres of African American music and has appeared in a number of anthologies and journals including *Journal of the Society for American Music, Black Music Research Journal, American Studies Journal, U.S. Catholic Historian* and *Musical Quarterly*. Her book *Soul on Soul: The Life and Music of Mary Lou Williams* is the most current biography on the jazz pianist/arranger. In 2011 she served as co-editor of the three-volume *Encyclopedia of African American Music* (ABC-CLIO), which is the first work of this genre to address all forms of African American music from 1619 until 2010. She also served as senior editor in the area of African American music for the revision of *New Grove Dictionary of American Music*. She has worked as a consultant with National Public Radio, The Kennedy Center for the Arts, Jazz@Lincoln Center and was the Scholar-in-Residence at the American Jazz Museum in Kansas City, Missouri from 1999–2001. In 2012, she was named as a scholarly consultant for the new National Museum of African American History in Washington, DC, that is slated to open in 2016.

Chamara (Sh'Mar'Rah) Jewel Kwakye (Kwa'Chee) is a Womanist scholar with interdisciplinary interests at the intersections of race, class, gender, sexuality and education; performance studies; ethnography; hip hop feminism; life histories; feminist pedagogy and girlhood studies. She has published works on qualitative methods, hip hop feminist pedagogy (*Wish to Live: The Hip-Hop Feminism Pedagogy Reader*, Peter Lang 2012) and is currently working on a monograph that examines the life histories of Black women in academia.

Denise Low-Weso, Kansas Poet Laureate 2007–2009, has been writing, reviewing, editing and publishing literary and scholarly articles for thirty years. She is the author of ten collections of poetry and six books of essays and a biography of Langston Hughes (co-authored with Thomas Pecore Weso). Low left Haskell Indian Nations University in 2012 after twenty-seven years as an administrator and faculty member. She now teaches classes for the School of Professional and Graduate Studies of Baker University as well as The Writers Place of Kansas City. She writes a regular poetry column for the *Kansas City Star*, and she is review editor of *Yukhika-latuhse* (she tells us stories), published by the Oneida Nations Arts Program. Individual members of the Associated Writers and Writing Programs elected Low to the national board of directors 2008–2013. She has served the board as conference chair and president (2011–2012).

Valerie Mendoza teaches in the American studies and history departments at the University of Kansas. She received her PhD in history from the University of California, Berkeley. Her research interests focus on Mexican Americans in Kansas, and she is completing a book manuscript titled *Beyond the Border: Gender and Community in Mexican Kansas City, 1900–1940*.